COMPLETE
CRAFT

COMPLETE CRAFT

Katherine Sorrell

PHOTOGRAPHY BY Howard Sooley

MURDOCH
BOOKS

PAINTING, PRINTING & DYEING 8   KNITTING & STITCHING 60

Contents

FELT 132   WEAVING & BEADING 154

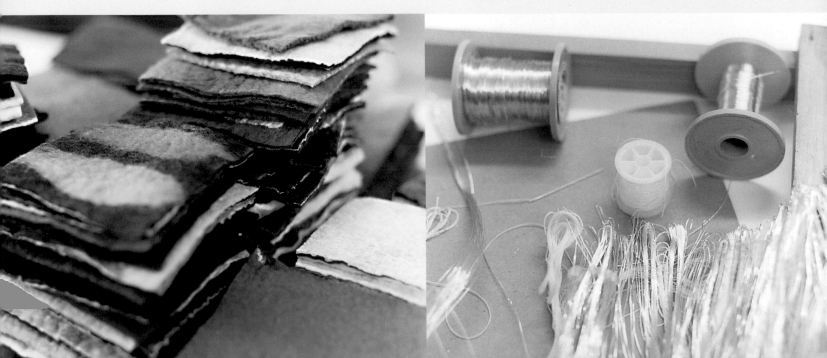

PAPER 196

CERAMICS & GLASS 228

METALWORK 260

CASTING & MOULDING 292

Introduction

It wasn't so long ago that people made things because they had to. Without 'craft' they wouldn't have had clothes to wear, implements to eat with, vessels to drink from, toiletries to wash with or bedlinen to sleep in. These days, of course, most of us can just pop out to the shops and buy more or less everything we need – we're 'cash rich, time poor' and there's no great necessity to spend hour after hour laboriously knitting, sewing, dyeing or weaving. So why is craft still so popular? Perhaps it's the very fact that we aren't obliged to do it that makes it attractive; perhaps it's the inherent satisfaction of being able to say 'I made that'; it could be because it's enjoyable for adults and children alike; or maybe it's just a basic human urge to create, to counteract the predominance of soulless, machine-produced items that normally surround us.

Certainly, craft has enjoyed a resurgence in recent years. For so long it was the object of scorn and derision, associated with lumpy, rustic, quirky pieces. But just as developing technology has resulted in the emergence of new craft forms, so traditional crafts have been revived and reinvented, and the result is that today's craftspeople frequently combine the best of old and new in a way that perfectly suits our eclectic, comfortable, modern homes. Craft may be highly functional or it may come close to fine art, but if it is well designed and well made it adds quality to our everyday lives. Craft has always been personal and meaningful, affordable and pleasurable; what is changed is that now it is also fashionable and inspirational.

This book is an exploration of the exciting possibilities of modern craft, demonstrating how one can take an ancient technique and adapt it to 21st-century living or, conversely, take a high-tech method and adapt it so the results are accessible. What makes this book unique is its breadth of coverage – we have selected 30 different types of craft, from the well-known (knitting, soap making, basketry) to the almost-forgotten (crochet, cyanotype, wirework) and the

cutting-edge (resin casting, acrylic moulding, complex textiles) and produced a pair of projects for each, resulting in 60 projects that range from table linen and jewellery to handbags and bowls, all of them very beautiful, highly desirable and eminently easy to live with.

Each project has been specially devised by a maker who is an expert in his or her field. And while you can see (and buy) their work in some of the world's leading galleries and stores, now you can also make your own version of their designs. It is possible to carry out each project on a kitchen table (or sometimes a garage or back garden) with the minimum of equipment and only a certain amount of dexterity. Some, naturally, require greater skill than others, but the clear, step-by-step photographs and written instructions, plus templates and, where necessary, more detailed instructions at the back of the book, should enable anyone to carry them out without too much difficulty. A comprehensive list of materials and equipment at the start of each project will also tell you what you will need to buy or prepare.

The other unique feature of this book is a concise history of each craft, which outlines how it arose and developed around the world. While it is not essential to know that the first beads probably date back to around 38,000BC, or that it was Roman legend that gave soap its name, it is, however, fascinating and illuminating, and will, hopefully, add an extra dimension of interest to your work. A blend of practical and intellectual is the ideal catalyst for craft, and this book provides a little of the latter alongside a great deal of the former, in a format that is both attractive and easy to follow. Explore one craft in depth (there's nothing to stop you developing your own ideas once you've mastered the techniques shown here) or learn numerous different ones – but, whatever you do, have fun with the process of making things and enjoy your gorgeously individual finished results.

one

PAINTING, PRINTING & DYEING

Stencilling

It is the very simplicity of stencilling that makes it such an effective and enjoyable craft – perfect for decorating surfaces large or small. But although the process is straightforward, the results can be wonderfully intricate and unique, as demonstrated by Japanese masters over the course of centuries.

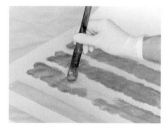

The practice of stencilling, or the art of painting repeated patterns through cut-out holes in a flat surface, has been around since prehistoric times, either to tell stories or just for decorative purposes. Cave-dwelling man produced stencil-like images of animals, and the ancient Egyptians used them extensively both inside and outside their elaborate tombs. The people of Fiji applied vegetable dyes onto bark cloth through primitive stencils cut from banana leaves, and in the Roman Empire stencils were first used commercially, to make the banners that advertized the popular games.

It was in 8th-century Japan, however, that stencilling was first given truly artistic form. The process was developed to such a superb level that amazingly fine details and intricate patterns became possible. In a technique known as *katazune*, expert craftsmen strengthened their cut paper – which could be so complex it resembled a web of holes with tiny, fragile links – with fine silk threads or hair. They used sheets of waterproofed paper made from mulberry fibre, in two layers at once – the threads or hair glued between them for extra support. The paper could be used several times, but when it became too damp, another stencil, exactly the same, was cut from a master, and registered using tiny pin holes. The colour was applied with a large, soft brush, or sometimes a rice-based resist paste was stencilled on and the cloth later immersed in a dye bath. Some fabrics were relatively simple; others were stencilled with many different patterns one after the other, and then embellished with hand-painting and embroidery for unsurpassed effect. This type of stencilling was the sole method of printing used in Japan until the 19th century. Elsewhere, meanwhile, more basic stencils could be found. The craft was brought to medieval Europe by returning Crusaders, and used for religious pictures and manuscripts, and also in grander manor houses for wall decorations, using rich colours and simple, repeated patterns – perhaps shields, crowns or *fleurs de lys*.

Similarly, stencils became a popular substitute for wallpaper in America during the late 19th and early 20th centuries. Not only were printed rolls of wallpaper expensive, but also stencilling (which was often carried out by travelling craftsmen) was a desirably unique and individual form of decoration. The method was also used for chairs, trays, boxes, bedspreads and other textiles, and there was a corresponding fashion for stencilled pictures, on a velvet background, of baskets of fruit and flowers.

In the 21st century, stencilling is still an admired craft. It may no longer be commonly practised professionally, but it is a means of producing patterns at home easily and inexpensively, using ready-made stencils or your own designs. On fabric, paper, walls, floors, furniture and accessories, the permutations of design and colour are practically limitless, whether simple or sophisticated, traditional or modern.

This glorious full-length curtain has a sumptuous feel, and the stencilled devoré effect is a clever way to diffuse light and disguise a window or a view.

Devoré curtain

you will need

- Felt-tipped marker pen
- Sheet of acetate
- Masking tape
- Cutting mat and craft knife
- Ruler
- Piece of dark blue or black cross-dyed silk/viscose velvet, long enough to cover your window and to allow 10cm at the top and bottom for hemming, and at least one-and-a-half times the width of the window. It should be pre-washed in a mild detergent to remove any finish
- Iron
- Pins
- Large printing surface (see page 15)
- Protective mask
- Light spray adhesive
- Overalls, apron or an old shirt
- Plastic gloves and protective goggles
- Stippling or stencil brush, or a small piece of sponge
- Ready-mixed devoré paste (about 500ml should cover one square metre of fabric)
- Mild detergent
- Sewing machine
- Thread to match the fabric

The devoré technique is ideal for making a curtain because, as seen so strkingly here, it can be used to create sheer and opaque areas through which the light is filtered in a series of fascinating and beautiful patterns. An excellent way to apply the devoré paste is through a stencil, as in this project, resulting in crisp edges and regular motifs. Choose any base colour you wish for the velvet, though darker shades will inevitably have the most impact.

1 2
3 4

how to make:
Devoré curtain

5

1 Photocopy to enlarge the stencil design on page 326 and then trace it onto the acetate. Tape to the cutting mat and cut out the squares and rectangles neatly with a craft knife. This is your stencil.

2 Press the velvet and, using pins or tape, attach it to your printing surface, pile-side down. Wearing a protective mask, lightly spray the stencil with adhesive and place on the fabric.

3 Wearing overalls, gloves and goggles, use the brush or sponge to apply the devoré paste through the stencil, brushing from the edges into the centre to avoid the paste leaking underneath. Apply the paste evenly all over, as thicker areas will devoré more and may cause holes in the fabric. Pull away the stencil carefully and reposition randomly, avoiding areas of wet paste, until you have covered the whole fabric.

4 When you have finished, wash your brush or sponge immediately and allow the entire piece of fabric to dry thoroughly. Then, wearing a protective mask and gloves, press the back of the fabric carefully with a hot iron for 30–60 seconds. Stop ironing when the fabric changes colour.

5 In a well-ventilated area, and still wearing a protective mask and gloves, gently rub the right side of the fabric so that the pile comes away and you can see the design. A stiff residue of paste will be left behind. Hand wash the fabric in warm water with a small amount of mild detergent. Rinse thoroughly in cold running water and allow to dry. Press the fabric and hem it neatly around all edges, then hang it at your window.

printing surface
Use chipboard or medium-density fibreboard covered with a blanket and a sheet of plastic, both stapled firmly to the underside of the wood and wrinkle-free.

alternative fabrics
You can buy other fabrics for devoré, such as silk, viscose, satin and polyester cotton – tell your supplier that they are for devoré techniques.

The luxury of suede is brought to life in this fabulous floor cushion. It's ideal for lounging on and is wonderfully fashionable in a casual, relaxed way.

Floor cushion

As modern interior design is influenced more and more by Eastern styles, we are increasingly eating, drinking and sleeping at a lower level. This superb floor cushion is not particularly either Eastern or Western in its design, but bridges the gap between the two in an unselfconscious, quietly luxurious way. The long, 'envelope'-style flap is another feature that gives the cushion a contemporary appearance, while the bold stripe design in silver adds just enough of a decorative element without going over the top.

you will need

(To make a cushion measuring 65 x 65cm)

- Sheet of wallpaper lining paper
- Ruler
- Pencil
- Scissors
- Masking tape
- Cutting mat and craft knife
- Piece of white suede (or leather), 67 x 195cm
- Large printing surface (see page 15)
- Tailor's chalk
- Light spray adhesive
- Overalls, apron or an old shirt
- Plastic gloves
- Protective mask
- Protective goggles
- Stippling or stencil brush, or a small piece of sponge
- Approx 500ml ready-mixed silver textile pigment dye
- Piece of calico or other light fabric
- Iron
- Sewing machine, with a leather needle
- Thread to match the suede
- Cushion pad, 65 x 65cm

how to make: **Floor cushion**

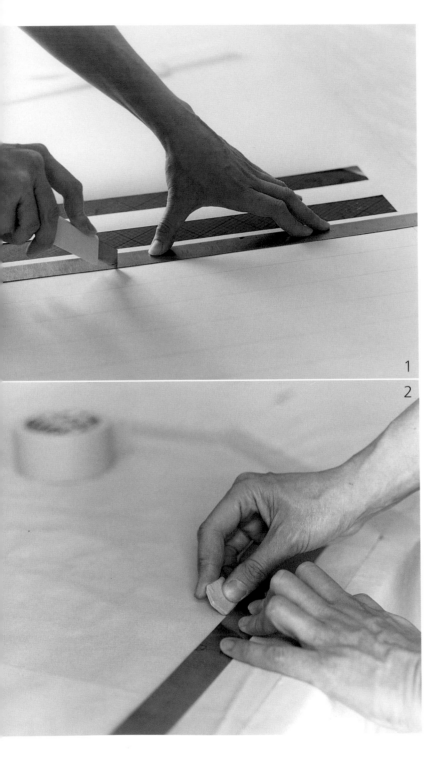

1

2

1 Cut a piece of lining paper 195cm long. Draw 21 rectangles within this larger rectangle, according to the template on page 327. Tape the paper securely to the cutting mat and cut out the rectangles neatly, using a craft knife. This is your stencil.

2 Using masking tape, attach the suede to your printing surface right-side up. With the tailor's chalk, draw two straight lines down each side of the fabric, 7.5cm in from the edges.

3 Place the cut stencil on the suede, lining up its edges with the two lines, and attach lightly with spray adhesive. Wearing the overalls, gloves, mask and goggles, use the brush or sponge to apply the dye evenly through the stencil, brushing from the edges into the centre to avoid the dye leaking underneath.

4 When you have finished, carefully pull away the stencil, wash your brush or sponge immediately and throw the stencil away. Allow the suede to dry thoroughly, then lay the calico over the back of it. Press the suede carefully with a hot iron, through the calico, for about 3–5 minutes to fix the dye.

5 Fold over one third of the suede, wrong sides together. Stitch neatly up each side, leaving a 1cm seam allowance. Cut away a narrow edge from the remaining third, on a slight diagonal, so that it forms a flap.

6 Cut two slits in the main body of the cushion, along the edges of one printed stripe, wide enough to insert the flap. Fill with the cushion pad and carefully tuck in the flap.

variations
You can vary this project by printing the stripes in different colours, or cutting them to different widths.

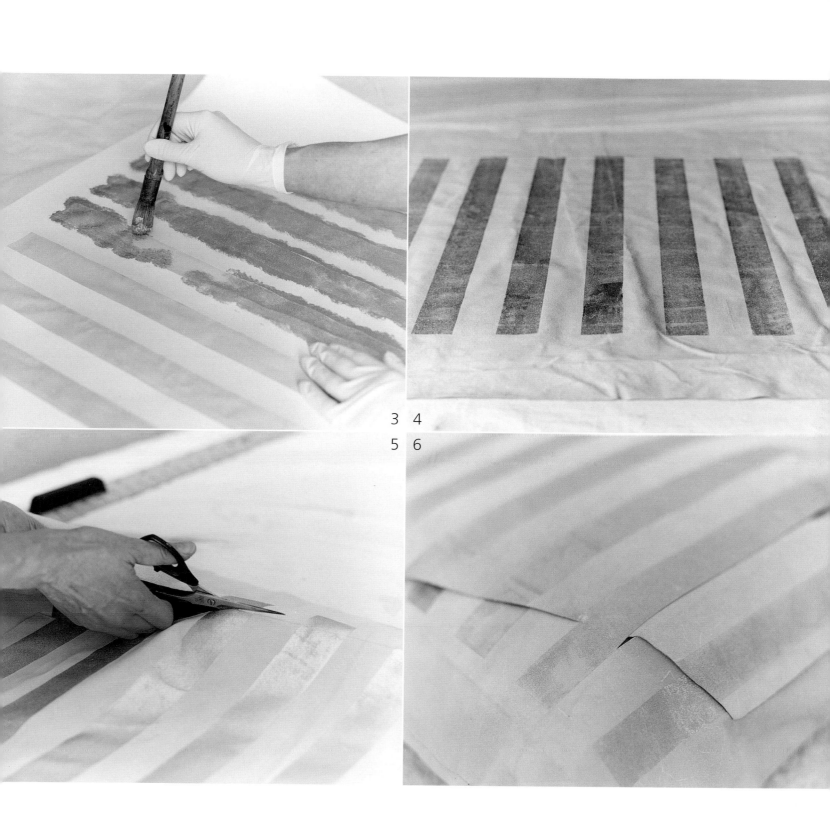

3 4

5 6

Screen printing

Most of the patterned fabrics we buy today have been industrially printed – a relatively new process that is fast, precise and hugely versatile. But screen printing by hand still has many advantages, enabling artists and craftspeople to produce images that are graphic, eye-catching and stunningly individual.

Patterning dyes onto fabric was a process carried out in ancient Greece, Rome and Byzantium, but the first real printing technique was almost certainly developed by the Chinese, who were printing paper with carved woodblocks two millennia ago. This, the oldest method of direct printing, has also been practised in India for centuries, in the form of vividly coloured and intricately patterned cottons, and was in use in medieval Europe as a minor textile craft. From woodblock printing came, in the late 18th century, a method of printing from engraved copperplates, particularly for the one-colour, scenic prints known as *toiles de Jouy*. From this developed the first mechanized printing process, cylinder (or roller) printing, which was patented in 1783 and revolutionized the Western textile industry, speeding up production to thousands of metres per day.

Screen printing is the youngest of all the direct printing methods, though it has a long and distinguished ancestry in the form of stencilling, to which it is closely related. But while stencilling can be wonderfully intricate and highly effective, it has the disadvantage of always requiring the 'ties' that link the cut-out patterns together. Screen printing was a refinement that no longer needed ties, thanks to the fact that the print is made by dye being pushed through a fine mesh held taut in a frame, with areas blocked out by paper stencils, varnish or photochemicals. It was in 1850 at Lyons that the first recorded stencil prints were made that were supported all over by silk gauze – though it is entirely possible that this process had been discovered in Japan long before. In 1907 an Englishman took out a patent for a 'tieless stencil' and during the First World War, posters and banners were produced by screen printing. But it was not until the 1920s that European and American screen printing became a viable industry, and the term 'serigraphy' was coined, from the Latin *seri*, meaning 'silk', and Greek *graphos*, meaning 'to draw or write'.

For several decades, screen printing remained a hand process, then in the 1950s the fully automated flat-bed screen printer came into operation, followed soon after by the rotary printer, both of which have made possible the printing of huge runs of fabric and paper in sophisticated, detailed and precise patterns of many colours. But the artistry of the hand screen print remains undiminished, and evidence of its qualities can be seen not only in the work of artists, including Andy Warhol, famous for his Marilyn Monroe and Campbell's Soup prints, but also in the ground-breaking designer fabrics produced by the European textile houses in the 1930s, '40s and early '50s. Colourful and creative, these fabrics epitomize all that is best about screen printing and show why it is still highly regarded today by artists, craftspeople, designers and couture houses.

Discreet but still effective, a paper wall hanging such as this makes an unusual and individual way to add character to a room, and is quick and easy to make.

Wall hanging

you will need

- Sheet of unprinted newsprint (or wallpaper lining paper), measuring 50 x 70cm, or the size of your screen
- Cutting mat
- Craft knife
- Ruler
- Masking tape
- Screen measuring about 50 x 70cm (see page 330)
- Roll of 1,200 or 1,400 grade lining paper
- Large printing surface (see page 15)
- Overalls, apron or an old shirt
- Plastic gloves
- Protective goggles
- About 500ml ready-mixed pearlized textile pigment dyes in each of two or three pastel colours
- Specialist screen-printing squeegee (see page 330)
- Brick (optional)
- Wallpaper paste, tacks or self-adhesive hook-and-loop tape

In this project, a choice of strong, hard, geometric shapes has been tempered by the use of pale, pearlescent colours, creating a wall hanging that would be delightful to install almost anywhere in the house (though it may not last too long in a bathroom or a steamy kitchen). Because the technique is so straightforward, once you feel confident with it you can develop your own shapes and patterns in order to tailor the design to the personality and style of your home.

how to make: Wall hanging

1 Put the newsprint on the cutting mat and use the craft knife to cut out a square within it – the square should be no longer than 50cm and no wider than 38.5cm. This will be the first stencil pattern (see page 326 for template).

2 Tape the stencil to the back of the screen, positioned so that a reservoir area of 10–15cm is created at one end of the screen. Hold the screen up to the light to check that all non-printing areas are covered by the stencil.

3 Tape the lining paper (either way up) to your printing surface and place the screen on it anywhere you like, allowing at least 20cm at the top for hanging. Wearing overalls, gloves and goggles, pour about 300ml of your first colour dye into one end of the screen.

4 Then, holding the frame with one hand and the squeegee with the other, pull the paste firmly and smoothly across the screen two or three times. Vary the angle of the squeegee and the pressure to apply more or less paste (the lower down the squeegee, the more ink you will squeeze through). You could place a brick on one end of the screen to hold it in place and use both hands.

5 Carefully lift the screen away from the paper and place elsewhere to start printing a pattern. You will need to print quickly to prevent the paste from drying on the screen.

6 After printing as many squares in this colour and size as you wish, scrape any excess paste back into the pot, throw away the paper stencil and clean the screen and squeegee under cold running water. Make another paper stencil in a smaller size and choose another colour, then repeat steps 2–5 to build up a varied pattern. If you decide to overlap any printing areas, ensure that the dye on the area you have already printed is dry. When you have decorated your desired area, neatly trim the lining paper top and bottom and allow to dry. Paste onto the wall as normal wallpaper, or use tacks or a strip of self-adhesive hook-and-loop tape.

3 4

5 6

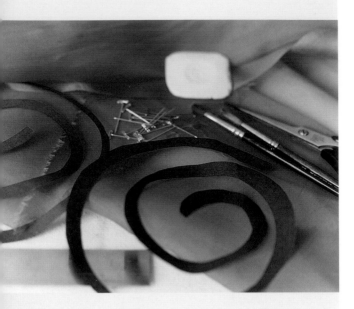

This pretty pink scarf in vivid magenta features a lovely spiral symbol. As it has been screen printed onto semi-transparent fabric, the result is a dazzling, multi-layered moiré look.

Spiral scarf

Long scarves in a striking sheer fabric are always useful and versatile, and the advantage of screen printing is that it enables you to cover vast lengths of fabric with the same design in no time at all. This project uses light-sensitive screen coating painted around a template, and employs a spiral motif that is highly stylish. But it would be just as easy to create a different pattern that could be printed to an equally fabulous effect.

you will need

(To make a scarf measuring 23 x 196cm)
- Pencil and pen
- Screen measuring 50 x 70cm (see page 330)
- Paintbrush
- 150ml light-sensitive screen coating
- Cerise silk organza measuring 50cm x 2m (washed in a mild detergent to remove any finish)
- Iron
- Masking tape
- Large printing surface (see page 15)
- Tailor's chalk
- Overalls, apron or an old shirt
- Plastic gloves and protective goggles
- 300ml ready-mixed acid textile dye (dark pink)
- Specialist screen-printing squeegee (see page 330)
- Piece of calico or other light fabric
- Tin foil
- Wok or pressure cooker
- Mild fabric detergent
- Pins
- Sewing machine
- Thread to match the fabric

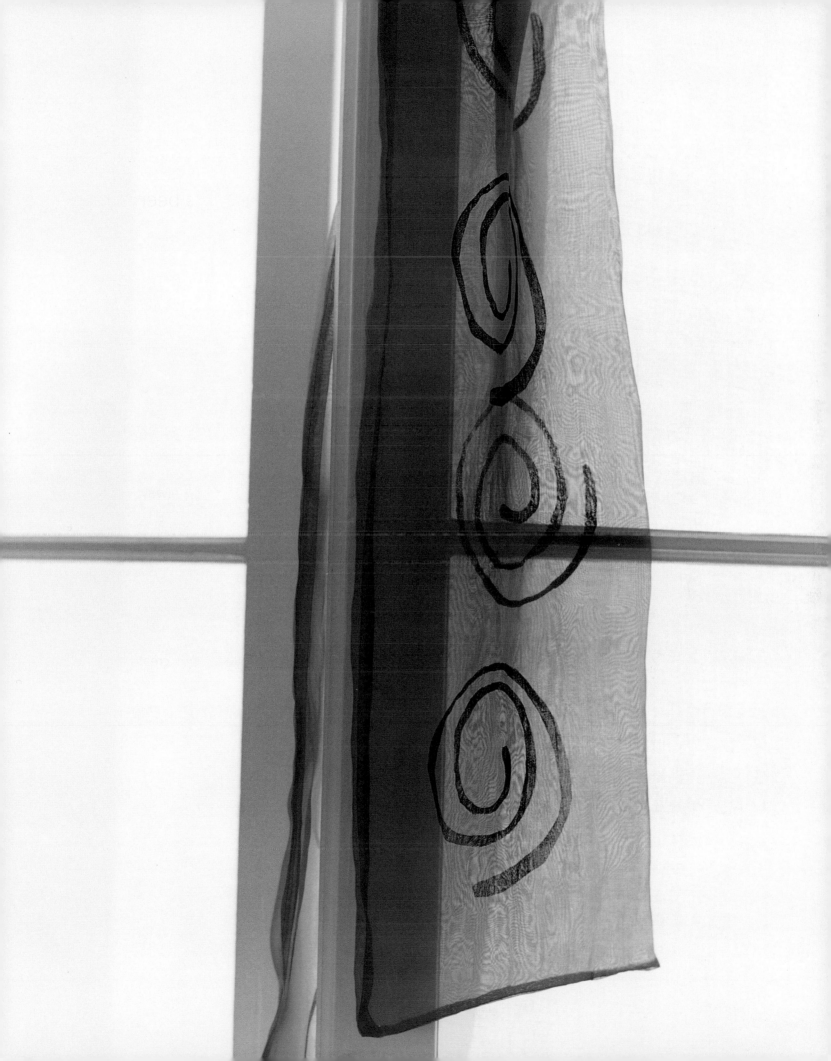

7

how to make:
Spiral scarf

1 Trace the template on page 325 onto the centre of your screen mesh. Paint around this with light-sensitive screen coating, leaving the design area unpainted. Allow to dry, then develop and fix it by leaving out in bright sunlight for 30–60 minutes until all the coating has changed colour. Ensure all of the non-design area mesh is covered in the emulsion, including a large enough reservoir space on the screen for the printing ink.

2 Press the fabric carefully and tape it, right-side up, to your printing surface.

3 Place the screen sideways at the top of the fabric and place masking tape to indicate the positions of the corners of the screen (stick the tape onto the printing base). Label these number 1. On both edges of the fabric, draw a short line with the tailor's chalk to indicate the top and bottom of the design area within the screen. Then move the screen along, judging by eye where the next printed design area should be. Indicate the corners of the screen again with masking tape and label as number 2. Repeat along the entire fabric, numbering 3, 4, 5 and so on.

4 Place the screen back into position number 1. Wearing overalls, gloves and goggles, pour about 250ml of the dye into one end of the screen (the reservoir area). Then, holding the frame with one hand and the squeegee with the other, pull the paste firmly, smoothly and evenly across the screen at least twice. Vary the angle of the squeegee and the pressure to apply more or less paste (the lower down the squeegee, the more ink you will squeeze through). If you find this hard, place a brick on one end of the screen to hold it in place, and use both hands to push and pull.

5 Carefully lift the screen away from the fabric and place within the registration marks numbered 3. Squeegee the ink across again. Continue printing alternate areas until you have covered the whole length of the fabric with the pattern. You will need to print quite quickly to prevent the paste from drying on the screen. When you have finished, scrape any excess paste back into the pot, wash the screen and squeegee under cold running water and leave the fabric and screen to dry. Then repeat step 4 to print the remaining alternate areas, starting with the tapes labelled 2, and so on. Clean the screen and squeegee again. (You can

use the screen again if you wish to re-print this pattern.) Leave the fabric to dry.

6 Detach the fabric and roll in the calico to make a sausage shape. Wrap the sausage in tin foil, sealing the edges. Place on a raised tray in the wok or pressure cooker with a small amount of water and steam for 30 minutes in order to fix the dye. Rinse in cold running water, then in hand-hot water with a small amount of mild detergent. Then rinse in cold running water again. Leave to dry completely.

7 Press the fabric with a warm iron, then fold over lengthways, right sides together, and pin. Leaving a seam allowance of 1cm, stitch around the long side and one of the short sides. Turn out, fold in the edges of the remaining side, iron and stitch neatly across. Press once more to finish.

---

re-using the screen

To reclaim the screen for re-use, you will need to buy some reclamation paste. Wearing rubber gloves, overalls and goggles, spread it over the side of the screen you do not squeeze through and leave for the manufacturer's recommended amount of time. Then, simply use a high-pressure washer to blast the old coating away from the mesh. As long as you are able to see through the mesh, you can re-use the screen.

Cyanotype

In cyanotype, a forerunner to photography, the appeal of vivid blue colour combines with the satisfaction of creating charming and unconventional images. The process has changed little since its invention in 1842, but today's practitioners are finding that it can be used in ways that add great vitality to the modern home.

A medium that has changed our perception of the world, photography was invented only 175 years ago. Its basic principles were discovered by four different men. In 1816 French physicist Joseph Nicéphore Niepce produced the first negative and, 11 years later, the first known photograph. Niepce worked with the painter Louis Jacques Mandé Daguerre who, in 1839, revealed his method of making a direct positive image on a silver plate, known as the *daguerreotype*. In England, scientist William Henry Fox Talbot was experimenting along similar lines, and had found a means of making endless positives from a paper negative, as well as of permanently 'fixing' images. His compatriot, astronomer Sir John Herschel, had also discovered a fixative, and was an early experimenter with photography on glass.

All four men were vital to the establishment of photography as we know it, and in 1844 the first book illustrated with conventional photographs was published – Talbot's *The Pencil of Nature*. But in this time of intense experimentation, various other photomechanical processes were discovered and explored, including one by Herschel himself – cyanotype. The process is similar to the experiments of Thomas Wedgwood and Sir Humphry Davy who, early in the 19th century, placed objects on paper soaked in silver nitrate and exposed them to sunlight, creating effective – though impermanent – black and white images. Herschel's method, however, employed light-sensitive iron salts, also known as Prussian Blue (hence cyanotype, from 'cyan', the Greek word for blue), rather than silver nitrate. It is believed that Herschel had been looking for a means of accurately copying his notes, drawings and calculations, and the resulting images were, literally, 'blueprints' of their subject matter.

Herschel made his discovery public in 1842, and in 1843 – one year before Talbot's book of photography – a book containing cyanotype images was published by Anna Atkins, a family friend of Herschel's, who had made nearly 400 prints of dried coastal algae. Quick, inexpensive and simple, cyanotype soon became a popular means of printing images on paper – for family portraits, artistic endeavours and in commerce (particularly for photographic proofs and for copying architectural and engineering drawings). As other photographic methods improved, however, cyanotype fell out of favour, though it was still widely used for architects' plans, thanks to the large-scale production of blueprint paper from the 1880s onwards.

Today, photographers, artists and craftspeople are once again experimenting with labour-intensive photographic processes, and have discovered the appeal and charm of cyanotype. Intriguing, individual and effective, the process can be applied to paper or to fabric, producing images that can be displayed as artworks or transformed into beautiful home accessories or even clothing.

The crisp contrast between the attractive blue of the cyanotype dye and the bright clean white of the fern outline is what gives this lampshade a unique and inspirational character.

Fern lampshade

you will need

- Overalls, apron or an old shirt
- Rubber gloves
- 18g ammonium ferric citrate
- 8g potassium ferric cyanide
- Small metal or glass bowl
- Measuring jug (metal or glass)
- Metal spoon
- Wide decorating paintbrush
- White cylindrical paper lampshade and sheet of heavyweight paper large enough to cover it
- Newspapers
- Board slightly larger than the paper
- Two or three dried fern sprigs
- Sheet of clear acrylic the same size as the board
- At least 4 clips
- Ruler
- Pencil
- Craft knife or scissors
- Spray adhesive
- All-purpose clear adhesive
- Ribbon to trim edges of shade
  (Any kitchen equipment should not be used for food afterwards)

The cyanotype process is now used for art and craft purposes rather than professional photography, but it has lost none of its charm and appeal. The technique itself seems almost magical, and you will find that you achieve different results every time, depending on the length of exposure, amount of sunlight and base colour of paper you work with. This project employs classic inky blue, trimmed with a contrasting ribbon, which brings out the detailing of the fern's silhouette with the utmost clarity.

how to make:
Fern lampshade

1 In a darkened room and wearing overalls and rubber gloves, mix the ammonium ferric citrate and potassium ferric cyanide in the bowl. Add 300ml of cold water and stir well until the chemicals have completely dissolved. This mixture is now light sensitive – do not expose it to light. It should be a pale yellowish-green colour.

2 Paint the solution evenly over the paper, protecting the surface underneath with plenty of newspaper, and allow to dry in the dark.

3 Still in a darkened room, put the dry, coated paper on the board, place the ferns evenly on the paper, and cover with the acrylic sheet. Clip the acrylic firmly to the board so that the fern is flat against the paper.

4 Take the board outside and expose to direct light. The longer you leave it, the darker the paper will become. About 20 minutes in average daylight will give a good image. In direct sunlight it may only take around ten minutes. Overcast days will require a longer exposure time. The paper will gradually turn a dirty grey colour. Bring the board back inside and remove the paper from the frame (discarding the ferns).

5 Develop the image by rinsing the paper well in cold water (wearing rubber gloves). Take care not to rip the paper – it will become quite fragile. Leave the paper, image side down, in cold water for five minutes, then carefully rinse off any remaining chemical until the water runs clear. The background will slowly turn blue, leaving a white image where the ferns were placed. Leave flat to dry (not in strong sunlight). Once dry, the image will be permanently printed.

6 Measure the lampshade and mark its dimensions on the printed paper, adding an overlap of 5mm on one vertical side. Cut out this shape.

7 Spray the back of the paper lightly with spray adhesive and carefully wrap the printed paper round the existing shade, gluing the vertical seam overlap.

8 To finish, glue ribbon around the top and bottom of the shade to give a neat edge.

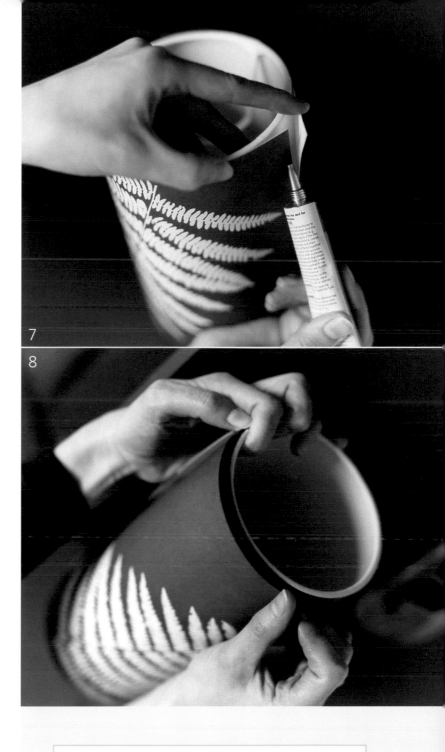

variations
You can make cyanotype prints in different colours. For purple, use a red paper and for green, use yellow.

Other leaves that are suitable for this technique include rosemary, ivy, bracken, eucalyptus and wild grasses.

Wonderfully practical yet beautifully decorative, this attractive floor cube blends science and nature to fabulous effect, and would make a striking addition to a living room or bedroom.

Feather floor cube

you will need

(To make a cube measuring 45 x 45 x 45cm)

- Four pieces of white or cream silk, each measuring 48 x 48cm
- Overalls, apron or an old shirt
- Rubber gloves
- 55g ammonium ferric citrate
- 25g potassium ferric cyanide
- Large metal or glass bowl or pan
- Measuring jug (metal or glass)
- Metal spoon
- Newspapers
- Board measuring 50 x 50cm
- Six or seven pigeon feathers or similar
- Sheet of clear acrylic measuring 50 x 50cm
- 4 clips
- Iron
- Pins
- Sewing machine
- Blue thread
- Scissors
- 1m heavyweight furnishing linen, in deep blue (at least 60cm wide)
- Cube of foam 45 x 45 x 45cm

(Any kitchen equipment should not be used for food afterwards)

The cyanotype process may be more than 150 years old, but used in this way it could not possibly look more modern. Although you could employ the same technique to make a cushion cover or perhaps a slip cover for a dining chair, the choice of a sculptural floor cube is ideal for a contemporary aesthetic. The cube's straight lines are offset by its rich metallic blue hue and the softness of the feathers; as an alternative, you could choose a more random or dense pattern, or try using feathers of varying shapes and sizes.

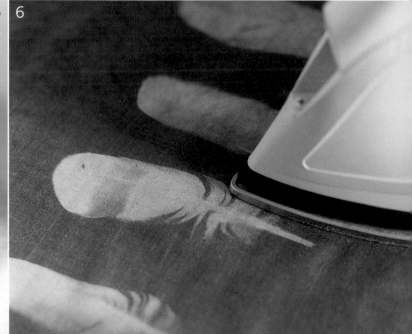

how to make:
Feather floor cube

1 Rinse the silk in warm water (to remove any residue or detergent). Squeeze out and leave damp.

2 In a darkened room and wearing overalls and rubber gloves, put the ammonium ferric citrate and potassium ferric cyanide together in the bowl or pan, add 800ml of cold water and stir well until the chemicals have completely dissolved. This mixture is now light sensitive – do not expose to light. It should be a pale yellowish-green colour.

3 Wearing gloves and still in the darkened room, dip the silk into the solution so that it is completely covered in the chemical, to ensure an even coating. At this stage you can either work on all four pieces of silk at once, or one at a time. Put newspaper on the floor to catch any drips, and hang the fabric up to dry, ensuring that it is taut and horizontal. When the fabric is dry – it will be a dark greenish-blue colour – put one piece on the board and place the feathers evenly on the fabric, then cover with the sheet of acrylic.

4 Clip the board securely to the acrylic, so that the feathers are completely flat against the fabric. Take the board outside and expose to direct sunlight. The longer you leave it, the darker the silk will become. Allow between 20 minutes and an hour, depending on whether it is bright sunlight or an overcast day.

5 Bring the board inside and remove the acrylic sheet and the feathers. Wearing rubber gloves, rinse the fabric under cold running water until the water runs clear. You may find it necessary to leave the silk in a bucket of cold water for some time to allow the residue chemical to leach out. When the feather images are white, the fabric is completely fixed. Leave to dry – once the fabric is dry it will be permanently printed. Repeat from step 3 with the other three pieces of silk.

6 Press the four pieces of printed silk and pin in a row. Stitch down the side seams, right sides together, allowing 1.5cm seam allowance, then join down the final seam to make a circle. Cut two rectangles of linen 30 x 48cm for the base of the cube and hem one long side on each piece. Press. Cut another piece 48cm square for the top of the cube.

7

8

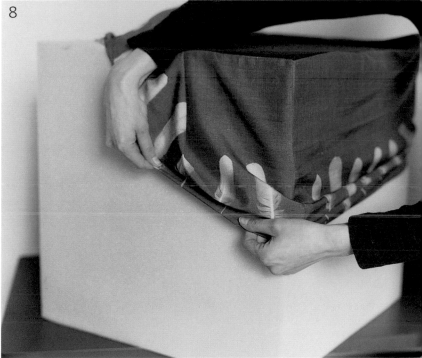

7 Pin the square of linen to the top edges of the circle of printed silk, with the right sides together, and stitch into place on a sewing machine to make a cube shape without a base.

8 To finish off, pin the hemmed linen rectangles to the bottom edge of the silk, right sides together and with the hemmed edges overlapping the centre, to make a base with a neat flap opening. Stitch the pieces together, then pull the finished cover carefully over the top of the foam cube. Smooth down the fabric so that it sits in place neatly.

Silk painting

For thousands of years, the secrets of sericulture, or silk cultivation, were closely guarded by the Chinese, who prized the luxurious fabric above all others. Strong, fine and glossy, silk is wonderfully wearable – and is the ideal fabric for sophisticated and creative decoration.

We have only legends to describe how the Chinese first learned to cultivate the silkworm, but it was probably at least 5,000 years ago. At first, the precious fabric, spun from the silkworm's cocoon, could be worn only by members of the royal family and their dignitaries, but gradually other classes were also permitted to wear silk, and it was used for home decoration and in commerce, too. In time, it became essential to the Chinese economy. Inevitably, it was also used as a form of money, too, and by the second century BC it was being exported along the trade route (known as the Silk Road) that linked East to West.

But the Chinese could not hold onto their monopoly forever. Despite capital punishment for anyone caught smuggling silkworms out of the country, it is thought that sericulture reached Korea around 200BC, India around 300AD and Byzantium around 550AD. By the Middle Ages it had reached Europe, and in Spain, France and England, silk was sought after by royalty and the aristocracy.

While man has decorated all types of fabric ever since he began spinning and weaving, it is silk that is most highly regarded for this purpose. Its texture, lustre and ability to absorb dye make it eminently suitable for painting and colouring. Ancient records indicate that textile dyes were used in China around 2,500BC, if not before. All over the world, however, different techniques were developed for colouring silk, from the block prints of India to the shibori (a sophisticated form of tie-dyeing, see page 50) techniques of Japan and the batik of Java. In fact, wherever silk was traded or cultivated, it was decorated in myriad ways. In Japan, in particular, silk decoration was developed to a particularly marvellous art form. Here, during the Middle Ages, shibori was sometimes combined with resist techniques, embroidery and free painting to create stunningly beautiful kimonos of immense complexity in pattern, though of extreme simplicity in cut.

Until the 19th century, of course, all dyes were made from vegetable, animal or mineral sources – madder red, saffron yellow and woad blue, for example. By 1900, however, a whole range of chemical-based colours had been developed, many of them more lightfast and easily washable than natural colourings. Since then, synthetic dyes have been widely used for silk decoration, creating intense, easy-to-use, permanent colours, whether for direct printing, resist work, free painting or immersion in a dye bath. Nowadays, some craftspeople are experimenting with natural dyes once again, while more types of synthetic dye are available than ever before. This makes the possibilities almost limitless for contemporary silk painters, who employ a wide range of traditional techniques but add a modern interpretation, to make the most of this ancient and beautiful fabric.

To add a decorative element to a room or simply brighten up a plain wall, a fabric hanging makes a wonderful change to a conventional painting, drawing or photograph.

Wall hanging

you will need

(To make a hanging measuring 85 x 110cm)

- Overalls, apron or an old shirt
- Rubber gloves, goggles and dust mask
- Length of satin silk pavona, 88 x 114cm
- 6 tablespoons soda ash
- Large plastic bucket (about 20 litres)
- Iron and pins
- Large printing surface (see page 15)
- Layout paper (9 x A3 sheets stuck together to the size of your hanging)
- Soft pencil and embroidery pen
- 10 tablespoons urea
- Measuring spoons and measuring jug
- 2 large (1 litre) plastic pots, one with a lid
- Mixing spoons or spatulas
- 1 teaspoon water softener (powder form)
- 4 tablespoons sodium alginate F
- Hand or electric whisk
- 40–50ml each of procion dyes (see right)
- 17 empty glass jars or plastic lidded pots
- Paintbrushes of various sizes, flat and round
- About 140ml water-based resist
- Hairdryer (optional)
- Newspapers (without colour pictures)
- Large saucepan with wire rack (steamer)
- Mild fabric detergent

If you love the look of silk painting, you will be unable to resist making this large wall hanging, which has a modern aesthetic without being in the slightest bit 'difficult'. Its simple, repeated shapes are calm and appealing, as are its muted colours, making it exceptionally easy to live with. And not only is the finished project lovely to look at, but also the technique of actually making the hanging – mixing the dyes, masking out areas and painting with soft brushes – is thoroughly enjoyable. This project uses dyes in the following colours: lilac, ice blue, brown rose, antique gold, bubblegum, pearl grey, navy, chocolate brown, midnight blue, warm black and bronze.

how to make:
Wall hanging

7

1 Wearing overalls, gloves, goggles and a dust mask, soak the fabric in the soda ash dissolved in 12 litres of water for 30 minutes, and leave to dry (unrinsed). Press, then pin to the print table, fairly taut.

2 Copy the design on page 326 onto the layout paper and pin it to the stretched fabric, allowing for a 2cm hem at the bottom and sides, and 4cm at the top. To transfer the design to the fabric, make holes through the paper with a pin along all the drawn lines at about 1cm intervals, then draw with an embroidery pen over the pierced lines. The design will be visible on the silk, defined by a series of dots.

3 Wearing the protective clothing, prepare the thickening paste by first dissolving the urea in 375ml of hot water. In the other pot, add the water softener to 500ml of cold water, then beat in the sodium alginate with a whisk. Add the urea solution to the alginate solution, beat together and leave to stand overnight, with the lid on.

4 Still wearing the protective clothing, prepare the dye stock solutions by adding 1 teaspoon of dye powder to 125ml hot water and mixing until completely dissolved. Store each dye stock solution in a separate lidded container, labelling the contents clearly. To mix the shades used in this project, add measured amounts of dye stock solution to measured amounts of thickening paste as follows: Lavender: 125ml paste, 1 teaspoon lilac dye stock, 1 teaspoon ice blue. Rose: 125ml paste, 2 teaspoons brown rose, 1 teaspoon antique gold, 2 teaspoons bubblegum. Beige: 125ml paste, 8 teaspoons pearl grey. Grey: 125ml paste, ½ teaspoon navy, 2 teaspoons brown. Light Brown: 125ml paste, 2 teaspoons antique gold, 2 teaspoons bronze, 5 teaspoons chocolate brown. Purple: 125ml paste, 4 teaspoons lilac, 2 teaspoons midnight blue, 1 teaspoon ice blue, 3 teaspoons warm black.

5 Paint the design, beginning with the ovals, spots and squares. Use smallish rounded brushes for outlining shapes and larger brushes for filling in. (For even results, fill in while the outline is still wet.) Let dry or use a hairdryer.

6 Paint resist over the ovals, spots and squares, so you can paint the large areas of colour without painting around all the shapes. Working like this also adds interest to resisted areas, as the background colour soaks through the resist in some places. Leave to dry (or use a hairdryer), then paint background areas and the border. Let dry again.

7 Roll the silk in newspaper, place in a saucepan with a wire rack, put a little water in the bottom and steam for 10 minutes with the lid on to fix the dye. Do this in a well ventilated area. Remove the fabric from the newspaper and rinse in cold running water, then in hand-hot water with a little mild detergent. Rinse in cold running water and let dry. Press when the fabric is still slightly damp. Hem the side and bottom edges by turning over once, pressing, and then pressing again with fusible hemming tape sandwiched between the fabric. For the top edge, press a 4cm hem, then press with the hemming tape so that there is a pocket of 2cm at the top edge in which to insert the dowel.

to finish, you will need:
- 4m fusible hemming tape
- Measuring tape
- 1.2 metres of 5mm dowel

A painted silk scarf is a beautiful object to own. This one can be dressed up or down as you wish, and is delightfully easy to wear.

Abstract scarf

you will need

(To make a scarf measuring 45 x 175cm)
- Overalls, apron or an old shirt
- Rubber gloves, goggles and dust mask
- Piece of crepe satin silk, 45 x 175cm
- 6 tablespoons soda ash
- Large plastic bucket (about 20 litres)
- Iron
- Pins
- Large printing surface (see page 15)
- Embroidery pen and/or coloured paper and scissors
- Measuring spoons and measuring jug
- 2 large (1 litre) plastic pots, one with a lid
- Mixing spoons or spatulas
- 10 tablespoons urea
- 1 teaspoon water softener (powder form)
- 4 tablespoons sodium alginate F
- Hand or electric whisk
- 10 empty glass jars or plastic lidded pots
- About 40–50ml each of procion dyes (see right)
- Paintbrushes of various sizes, flat and round
- About 140ml water-based resist
- Hairdryer (optional)
- Newspapers (without colour pictures)
- Large saucepan with wire rack (steamer)
- Fabric detergent and fabric softener
- Needle and thread to match main colour

If you've been put off trying silk painting because of its frequent emphasis on 'artistic' imagery and vivid colours, this project is an introduction to the craft that takes a more contemporary, understated approach. Simple geometric shapes are repeated in a small range of soft colours, making for a design that has just as much validity as traditional silk painting, but a much more modern style. Vary the colours if you wish to coordinate with your wardrobe, but bear in mind that subtle shades are best. This project uses the following colours: antique gold, bronze, chocolate brown, navy, ice blue, midnight blue and warm black.

how to make:
Abstract scarf

For safety guidelines, see page 45.

1 Wearing overalls, gloves, goggles and a dust mask, soak the fabric in the soda ash dissolved in 12 litres of water for 30 minutes and leave to dry (unrinsed). Press, then pin to the print table, fairly taut.

2 Plot out your design on the fabric, using an embroidery pen and/or cutting out shapes in coloured paper. If you wish, you can copy the design on page 326.

3 Wearing the protective clothing, prepare the thickening paste by first dissolving the urea in 375ml of hot water. In the other pot, add the water softener to 500ml of cold water, then beat in the sodium alginate with the whisk. Add the urea solution to the alginate solution, beat and leave overnight with the lid on.

4 Still wearing all your protective clothing, prepare the dye stock solutions by adding 1 teaspoon of dye powder to 125ml hot water and mixing until completely dissolved. Store each solution in a separate lidded container, labelling the colours clearly. To mix individual shades, add measured amounts of dye stock solution to measured amounts of thickening paste as follows: Light brown: 125ml thickening paste, 2 teaspoons antique gold dye stock, 2 teaspoons bronze dye stock, 5 teaspoons chocolate brown dye stock. Light blue/grey: 125ml thickening paste, 2 teaspoons warm black, 3 teaspoons ice blue. Dark blue: 125ml thickening paste, 1 teaspoon warm black, 2 teaspoons navy, 4 teaspoons midnight blue, 1 teaspoon chocolate brown, ½ teaspoon antique gold.

5 Paint the areas to remain white (the rings and stripes) with resist. Paint the coloured spots and stripes with thickened dyes. Use smallish, rounded brushes for outlining shapes, and larger brushes for filling in. (Fill in before the outline dries or the brushstrokes will show.) For neat stripes, use a flat brush; for looser stripes, a rounded brush. Let dry or use a hairdryer.

6 To paint the background colour of the areas patterned with spots, paint resist over each spot then, using a large flat brush, paint over the area to be coloured. On patterned areas reserved white with the resist, paint the background colour over the resisted areas.

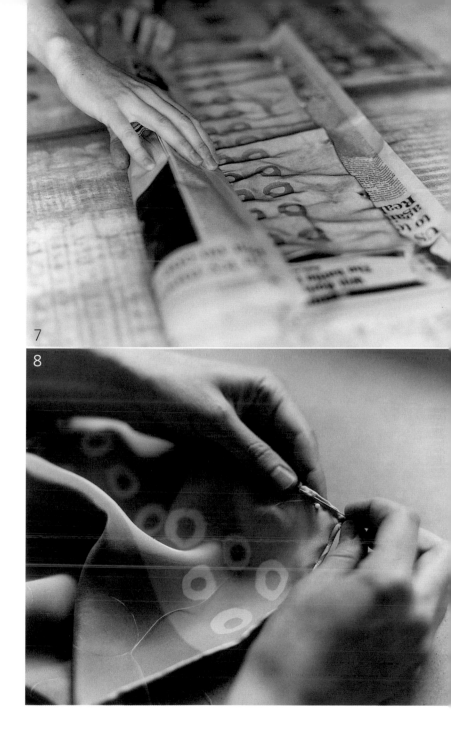

7

8

7 Roll the scarf in sheets of newspaper, place in a large saucepan with a wire rack, put a small amount of water in the bottom and steam for 10 minutes with the lid on to fix the dye. Do this in a well-ventilated area away from areas used for food preparation. Remove the fabric from the newspaper and rinse, first in cold running water, then in hand-hot water with a small amount of mild detergent. Then rinse in cold running water again. Soak in fabric softener and rinse again. Leave to dry.

8 Press when the fabric is still slightly damp, and hem the edges by rolling over twice, pinning, then stitching by hand with small hemming stitches.

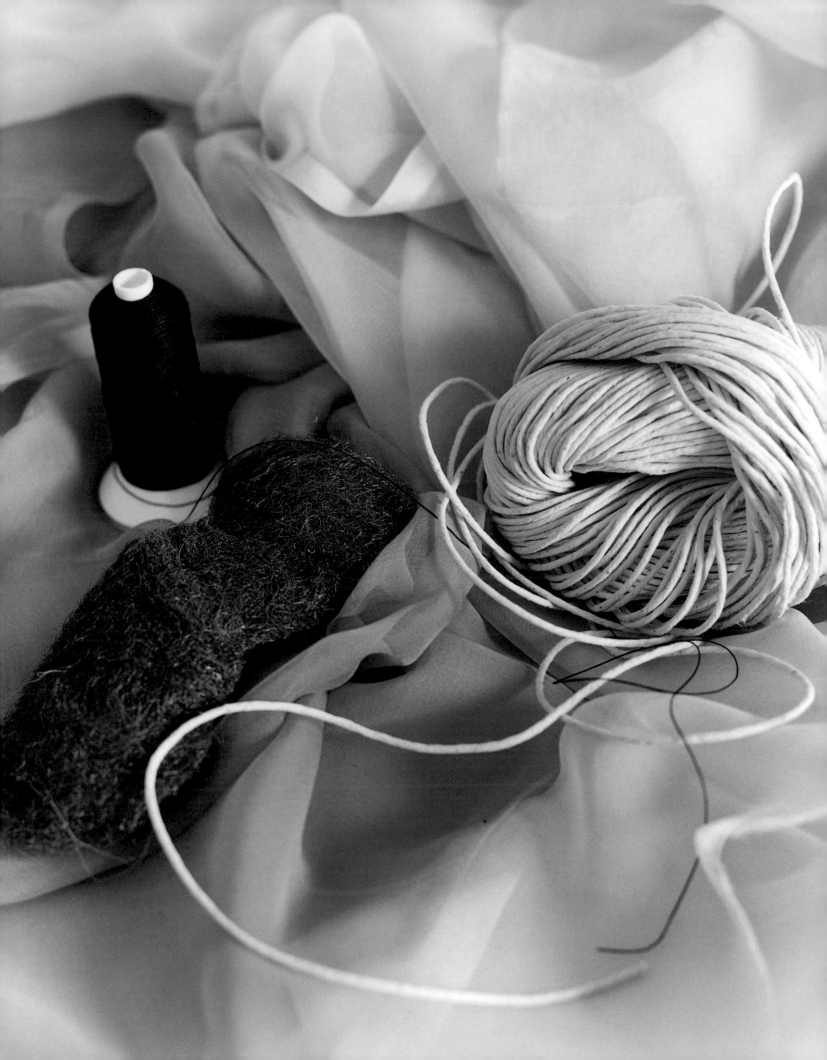

Shibori

The practice of tying and dyeing fabric has been around for many years and in many countries – sometimes from the need to re-use old cloth; sometimes for the beauty of the effect. Shibori-dyed fabric is especially appealing – its traditional patterns are centuries-old, but its attraction is fresh, modern and exciting.

Shibori is the Japanese word for resist-dyed textiles that have first been shaped, perhaps by folding, plaiting, crumpling or twisting, and then secured, by stitching, knotting or binding. What makes them so special is their pretty soft-edged patterns, which appear completely different from the sharply dyed edges that result from using resists of wax, paste or stencils. And like all dyeing processes, there is an element of chance in the method – depending on how the fabric is shaped, the strength of the dye and the length of time in the dye bath – which gives a wonderfully lively, characterful appearance.

The oldest known shibori cloth was discovered in Peru, and dates back to the first or second century BC. At different times, shibori has been made in Ecuador, Guatemala, Bolivia, Paraguay, Argentina and Mexico, involving fine, hand-woven woollen and cotton cloth. In India, shibori was practised mainly in western areas, using muslin or silk, often with hundreds of tiny spots forming patterns on a dyed background, and used for saris, veils and turbans. There it was (and still is) known as *bandhana* work; in Indonesia, another important tie-dye area, it is called *plangi* (bound cloth) and *tritik* (stitched cloth), depending on the specific technique involved. Silk was generally the base fabric, perhaps bound and sewn with

leaf fibres and intricately dyed in colourful, contrasting colours. The nomadic tribes of North Africa dyed simple spot and circular patterns onto woollen loincloths, and it is thought that the Bedouin and Berber people passed on their knowledge to other areas of the country. The processes were developed over the years, and today shibori is still flourishing in West Africa. For the Yoruba people of West Nigeria it is called *adire*, and is dyed with indigo to create magnificently patterned cloth.

While shibori has been practised all over the world for centuries, it is in Japan that it has been most fully explored. It is believed that shibori reached Japan from China around the end of the sixth century, after which it developed rapidly and became particularly fashionable among the aristocracy. During the Middle Ages it was more widely available, reaching an unprecedented level of popularity, used for samurai garments, government officials' uniforms and ordinary people's clothing. A wide variety of complex techniques was developed, which required an extraordinary amount of skill, so shibori dyers were respected and admired members of society.

Today, shibori is still a living craft in Japan, widely practised commercially and now entering new areas. Until recently it was used mainly for kimonos, but it is now being applied to fashion accessories such as scarves and wraps, and to interior items including bed covers and lampshades, demonstrating the virtuosity of its makers and the magical effects of this intriguing craft.

Wonderfully floaty and feminine, this scarf possesses both delicacy and a bold, striking design – the result of a technique that is ancient in form, but thoroughly modern in aesthetic.

Monochrome scarf

you will need

(To make a scarf measuring 50 x 50cm)

- 50cm square piece of white silk georgette or fine silk
- Weighing scales
- Fabric detergent (liquid)
- 50cm length of smooth, rigid, plastic pipe or tube, about 15cm in diameter
- Wire wool
- Furniture polish
- Ball of string
- Strong thread
- Scissors
- Overalls, apron or an old shirt
- Rubber gloves
- Protective mask
- Packet of black dye (cold dye is ideal)
- Two plastic buckets (one stainless steel, if heat is required for the dye)
- Fabric conditioner
- Iron
- Needle (or sewing machine)
- Thread to match the dye colour

Some tie-dyed fabrics can appear a little clumsy and unsubtle, but if you employ the shibori technique with a certain dexterity, as demonstrated here, you can achieve a look that is superbly impressive and absolutely sophisticated. The visual intrigue of this appealing project lies in its bold juxtaposition of graphic black and white stripes, delicately narrow and pleasingly irregular. This is a vibrant design that would be worn equally well with either a casual outfit or a smart business suit.

1 2
3 4
5 6

how to make:
Monochrome scarf

1 Weigh the silk in order to determine how much dye to use. Hand wash it in hand-hot water with a little detergent to remove any finish, and spin to remove excess water. Also ensure that the pipe is really smooth by polishing with wire wool and furniture polish.

2 Roll the damp fabric around the pipe at 45 degrees to form a diamond shape. To hold the silk in place while it is wrapped, tie the ends and the centre with string. Take the strong thread and knot around the base of the pipe.

3 Holding the pipe in one hand, firmly wrap the thread around the silk, leaving about 2cm between each line of thread (the further apart the thread, the more fabric will be exposed to the dye). After about 10cm, push the fabric down (towards the end of the pipe) to form concertina folds. Remove the string when the thread reaches it.

4 Continue wrapping the thread until all of the fabric is condensed into folds. Cut off the thread and knot securely. Soak the wrapped fabric in tepid water for an hour.

5 Wearing overalls, rubber gloves and a mask, mix up the dye in the bucket, following the manufacturer's instructions and observing safety recommendations. Make sure there is enough water to cover the fabric on the pipe. Place the pipe in the dye bath. Leave in for the recommended length of time to give a strong colour, moving the pipe around a little occasionally to prevent the dye from settling.

6 Remove the pipe from the dye and rinse away excess dye under the cold tap. Carefully unwind the fabric from the pipe, discarding the thread.

7 Thoroughly rinse the fabric with cold water until the water runs clear. Hand wash and condition the fabric in a bucket full of hand-hot water, and leave to dry.

8 Press the fabric. To hem the edge by hand, fold over the raw edges about 1cm. Start with the needle at the raw edge and make a couple of stitches to secure the thread. Slip the needle into the fold and run it along inside for 1–2cm. Take it out and pick up a tiny piece of the fabric just below the exit beside the raw edge. Repeat by putting the needle into the fold again, just beside where it came out. Continue all the way round to give a good rolled hem. Alternatively, you could machine stitch the hem.

7

8

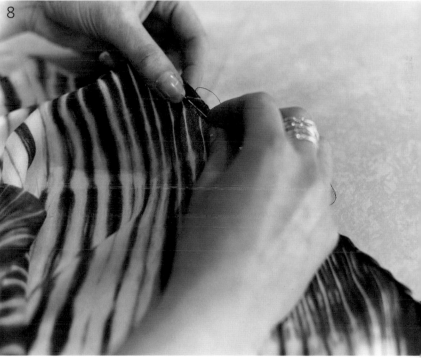

wrapping the thread
When you wrap the length of thread around the pipe, make sure that you keep the tension fairly taut. If you wrap it round too loosely, the dye will get under the thread and you will not achieve the desired striped effect.

The subtlety of the shibori technique has to be seen to be believed, and this throw is an utterly glamorous example of just how beautiful and impressive it can be.

Velvet throw

you will need

(To make a throw measuring about 2m x 110cm)

- 2m white velvet, at least 110cm wide
- Weighing scales
- Sewing machine
- Fabric detergent (liquid)
- Tacking thread
- Needle
- Scissors
- Ball of string
- Weights
- Quilting thread
- Overalls, apron or an old shirt
- Rubber gloves
- Protective mask
- Packet of dark petrol dye (ideally cold dye)
- Small glass jar
- Plastic bucket (stainless steel, if heat is required for the dye)
- Fabric conditioner
- 2m satin at least 115cm wide
- Pins
- Silk thread to match the velvet
- Iron

The delicious deep slate grey of this soft velvet combines perfectly with its irregular shibori-dyed pattern to create an irresistible piece that is almost decadent in its luxury. Other colours could have an equally eye-catching effect, depending on the décor you would like them to match – a deep red, perhaps, or emerald green, midnight blue, dove grey, pale lilac or a burnt orange. Alternatively, for a very unusual effect, try the same technique using several shades of a colour and cut the fabric into smaller pieces to create a beautiful patchwork quilt effect.

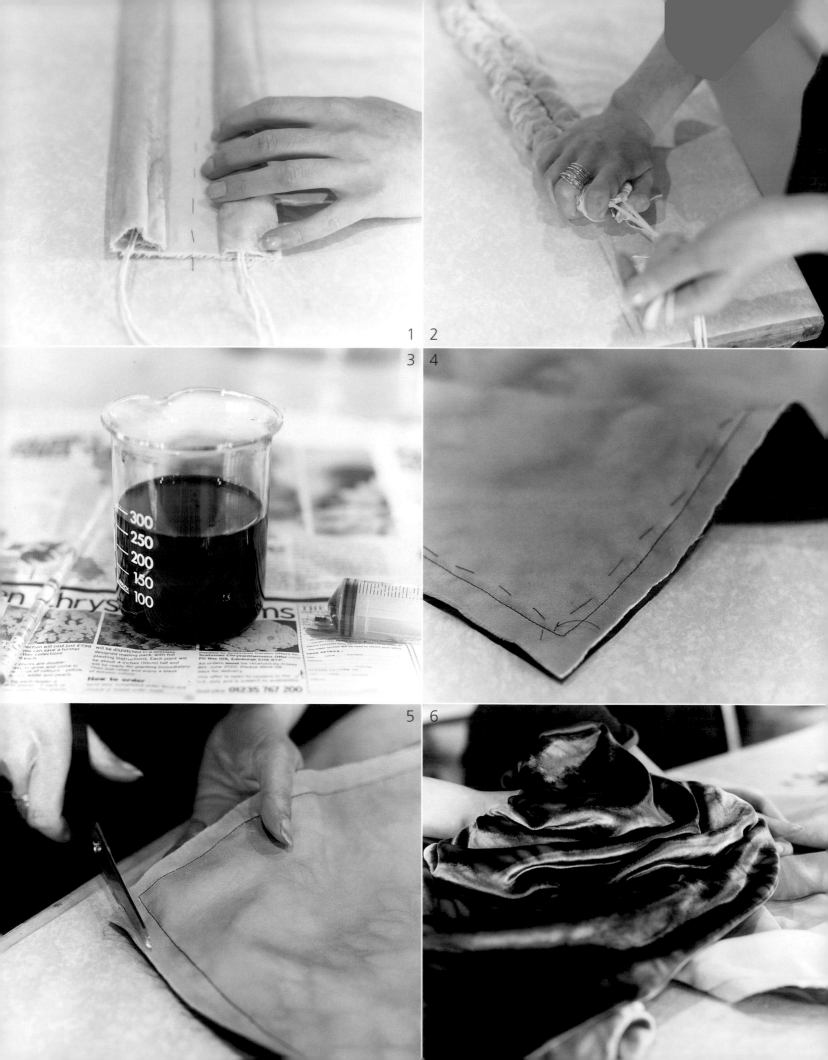

how to make:
Velvet throw

1 Weigh the velvet in order to determine how much dye to use. With the sewing machine, overlock the edges of the velvet so that it does not fray, then machine wash (on a low temperature, using a gentle cycle) to remove any finish. Spread the damp velvet right-side down on a large table. With tacking thread, mark the centre lengthways. Cut a double length of string and lay it along one of the long edges. Starting at the edge, roll the fabric around the string. Continue rolling until you reach the tacking thread in the centre, then use weights to hold the rolled velvet in place. Repeat from the other side.

2 Tie short lengths of quilting thread loosely around the double sausage-shaped fabric, leaving gaps of about 5–10cm between them, all the way along. At one end, take the ends of the 'core' string and tie them together firmly. At the other end, hold both of the core strings in one hand and with the other hand push the fabric so it wrinkles up. When the fabric has been concertina'd, tie the core strings securely. Submerge in lukewarm water for at least an hour.

3 Wearing overalls, gloves and a mask, mix up the dye in a glass jar, following the manufacturer's instructions and observing any safety recommendations, then pour into the bucket. Place the fabric in the dye bath. Leave until the dye has produced a strong colour, stirring regularly. Once dyed, rinse thoroughly under cold running water. Untie, wash (as in step 1) using fabric conditioner, spin and let dry.

4 Cut off the overlocked edges of the velvet, then place it on top of the satin, right sides together, and pin around all the edges. Tack over the pins about 2cm from the raw edge. Remove the pins.

5 Cut the satin to the size of the velvet (the velvet may have shrunk). Machine stitch 1.5cm from the raw edge, leaving a gap of about 15cm in the middle of one long side. Remove the tacking and trim excess fabric from the corners.

6 Turn out. Press the edges flat, taking care not to crush the pile, and neatly hand stitch the opening together.

7 Lay the throw out completely flat. In its centre, pin through both layers. Then pin again, working from the centre at 25–30cm intervals both horizontally and vertically, to produce a grid shape of pins.

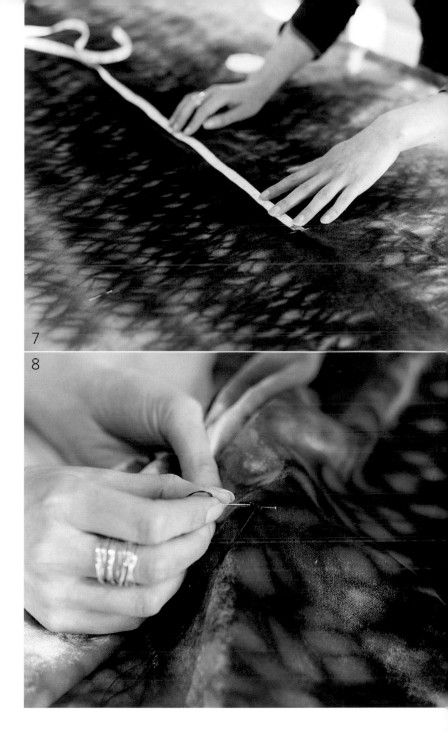

7

8

8 Thread a needle with a double length of silk thread. At one of the pinned points, make two small stitches on top of each other through both layers (starting at the reverse of the throw), leaving a tail of thread when you start and finish. Tie the two tail ends together, being careful not to distort the fabric by pulling too tightly. Trim the ends to about 1.5cm (if you cut them too close to the fabric they may come undone). Do not worry about leaving loose threads on the reverse of the quilting – this is a traditional feature of quilting and will give your work authenticity. Work over the entire throw, removing the pins as you go.

two

KNITTING & STITCHING

Knitting

While the basic knitting stitches are extremely simple, this is a craft that can be used to create fabrics in which colour, pattern and form combine in the most complex and harmonious ways. Useful, everyday items can be plain and unassuming or highly sophisticated, creative works of art.

The word 'knit' comes from the Old English *cnotta*, 'knot', but it is not a traditional English technique. In fact, it is thought that knitting originated in the Middle East (possibly among the Arabian nomads), and from there spread across North Africa and to Spain. By the 10th century it was certainly a well-developed craft, as demonstrated by the complex knitted socks that have been discovered in Egyptian tombs.

Various portraits of a 'knitting Madonna' show that knitting had reached Europe by the 14th century, and by the 15th and 16th centuries it was a well-established commercial business. It was organized into men-only guilds of professionals, who made caps, stockings and other knitted articles for the domestic market and for export. While the aristocracy enjoyed fine silk knitwear, perhaps a shirt, gloves or even a cushion, the less well-off knitted their own, more humble garments, giving rise to distinctive community knitting styles such as fishermen's ganseys (close-fitting sweaters with distinctive monochrome patterning) and, later, Fair Isle and Arran knits. Then, in 1589, English clergyman William Lee invented a knitting machine that could work 100 times faster than any hand-knitter (interestingly, the modern machine differs little from Lee's centuries-old design in its basic technology). At first Lee's invention could only deal with thick, woollen yarn, but eventually it was refined to cope with silk and to produce intricate patterns. This led to a cottage knitting industry in Britain, in which families rented out a hand-frame machine, the children wound the yarn, the men operated the machine and the women sewed up the garments. This thrived until the Industrial Revolution.

In the 18th and 19th centuries, meanwhile, thanks to increased prosperity and leisure time, combined with rigid views on how women should conduct themselves, hand knitting (along with embroidery) gradually transformed from being a poor person's necessity to a rich woman's pastime. Refinements were made – needles were given capped ends, for example – and printed patterns became extremely popular, often for small accessories such as pen-wipers or pincushion covers. In the 20th century, even after the emancipation of women, hand knitting continued to be a popular hobby, a satisfying creative outlet, inexpensive and useful. Women knitted all sorts of items – from baby clothes and sweaters to underwear and entire coats. But it was not until the 1960s and '70s that there was an explosion of knitting as a real craft form, when art students discovered its potential and began to experiment, combining unusual stitches, mixing yarns of different types and textures and taking inspiration from fine art for pattern and colour. Since then, knitting has been seen as fashionable, ingenious and experimental. Its basic stitches may be linked to the past, but fresh ideas and interpretations have given it an adventurous, exciting future.

Experience the comfort of a giant, plump cushion, knitted in softest merino wool. Its neutral colour ensures that this project will complement any style of décor.

Chunky cushion

you will need

(To make a cushion measuring about 50 x 50cm)

- Saw
- 2 broom handles (about 2.3cm diameter)
- Ruler or measuring tape
- Sandpaper (optional)
- Glue (optional)
- 2 discs/knobs (optional)
- Small amount of olive oil (optional)
- 3 kilos thick, unspun cream merino wool yarn (tops – 64 quality)
- Steam iron
- Scissors
- Cushion pad 50 x 50cm
- 2 buttons
- Large-eyed needle
- Twine

(See page 328 for instructions on how to knit)

Hand knitting may not currently be in its heyday, but the satisfaction that one can gain from this classic domestic craft is just as great as it ever was. Though the skill is traditional, the results can be anything but; this cushion, for example, is overscaled in both its dimensions and its wonderfully chunky rib – which is achieved by using broom handles instead of conventional needles. The finishing touch is a pair of mother-of-pearl buttons, whose iridescence provides a contrast to the texture of the wool.

1 2
3 4

how to make:
Chunky cushion

1 Saw the broom handles to about 70cm long each so you can use them as knitting needles. If necessary, sand the rounded ends with sandpaper. It will make knitting easier if you glue discs or a door knob to the ends to stop the knitting dropping off. It will also be easier to knit if you lightly oil the 'needles' with olive oil.

2 Practise knitting with the needles and thick yarn until you are used to the feeling. As you wrap the yarn around the needles, twist it slightly. This sample can be easily unravelled and the yarn used again.

3 To make the cushion, cast on enough stitches for a 55cm width. Then knit, using stocking stitch (one row knit, one row purl), for 110cm, slipping the first stitch of each row except the first row (transfer the stitch from the left to the right needle without working it). Cast off loosely on a purl row.

4 Press flat with a steam iron and fold the knitting in half lengthways. Cut a 1.5m length of the yarn and neatly join the two sides together, using your fingers to push the yarn in and out of the knitted stitches, as if you were using a needle and thread.

5 Insert the cushion pad. Attach the buttons to a length of twine and stitch to one open side. Fasten, using a stitch as a buttonhole. Press with a steam iron.

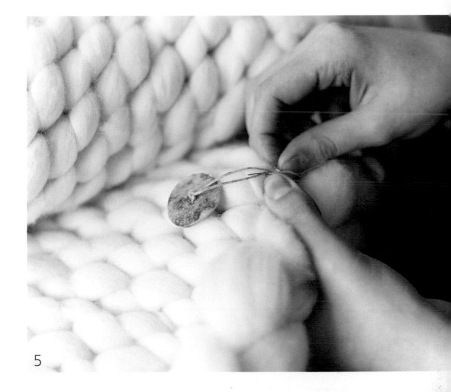

5

joining wool
When you are joining two lengths of wool, just leave a long end of wool (about 15cm) from your knitting and join on the new ball alongside – knit the two lengths of wool together until the first one runs out.

This cute little knitted bag – with a delightful raspberry-ripple effect – slips neatly over the shoulder for a look that is both fun and casual.

Casual bag

you will need

(To make a bag measuring about 24 x 30cm)

- One hank (350g) natural merino wool roving (prespun wool), wound into two balls
- One hank (350g) raspberry ripple, space-dyed merino wool roving, wound into two balls
- Pair 15mm knitting needles
- Fabric detergent and conditioner
- Measuring tape or ruler
- Iron
- Sewing machine
- Thread to match the wool
- Piece of linen measuring 26 x 58cm
- Needle
- Pins
- Button

(See page 328 for instructions on how to knit)

No one could argue that this sweet handbag is too formal – in fact, its chunky ribbed texture and slightly uneven shape make it just right for a walk in the park or a relaxed weekend in the country. Once you've got the hang of the project's basic principles, you could easily adapt its height, width and, of course, colour, to match any outfit in your wardrobe. The bag fastens with a simple button pushed through the stitches; a nice alternative might be a small toggle or maybe a leather knot.

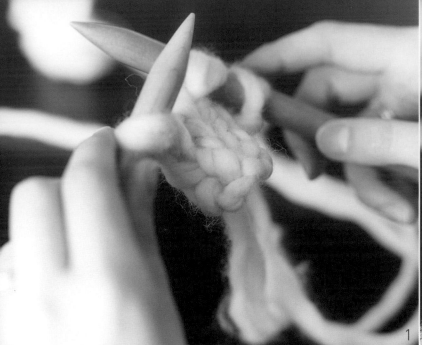

1

2

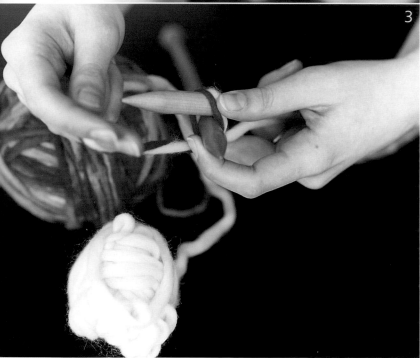

3

4

5

6

how to make:
Casual bag

1 Using two strands of roving, knit a sample swatch 10cm square and count the number of rows and stitches. Felt the square (see step 4) and, when dry, measure its size in order to establish both the tension and how the felting affects the wool. From this, work out the number of stitches and rows you will need to knit for this project. (As a general guide, you will need to knit the bag a little bigger to allow for the felting, but all wool behaves slightly differently so it is necessary to check. If the bag does not come out to the exact measurements given here, remember to adjust the size of the lining accordingly.)

2 Using two strands of natural roving, cast on enough stitches to make a finished (after felting) width of 26cm. Knit, using stocking stitch (one row knit, one row purl), to make a finished length of 10cm. Break off one strand of natural, leaving about 15cm of wool, and tie in a pink strand. Continue for a further finished length of 10cm. Break off the second strand of natural and tie in the second strand of pink. Continue, using two pink strands, for a further finished length of 20cm.

3 When the total length is equal to a finished length of 40cm, break off one pink strand and tie in a natural strand. Knit for a finished length of 10cm. Break off the second pink strand and tie in the second strand of natural. Continue, using two natural strands, for another finished length of 10cm, until the total length is equivalent to a finished length of 60cm. Cast off on either row.

4 Gently felt the knitted rectangle by washing in hot, soapy water and kneading it for a few minutes, until you feel the quality of the fabric change. Rinse with cold water. Repeat if necessary. Add fabric conditioner and rinse again. Spin in a washing machine and dry flat, pulling the knitting into shape while still wet. The bag should shrink to 26 x 60cm. (For more information on felting, see page 139.)

5 Fold the knitted rectangle in half, right sides together, and press. Allowing 1cm for the seams, machine stitch the two long sides together.

6 Take the linen and stitch a 3cm hem at each of its short ends. Fold in half, right sides together and stitch the two long sides together, allowing 1cm for the seams. Turn out.

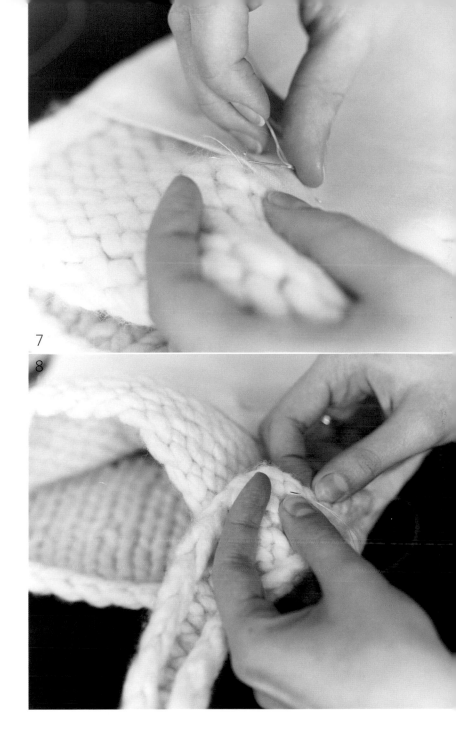

7

8

7 Place the knitted bag (inside out) inside the linen bag – it will protrude by 4cm. Hand sew the lining to the knitting at the top and turn out. The top edge will curl over.

8 Using two strands of natural roving, knit a strap 5 x 80cm, casting on an uneven number of stitches. Slip the first stitch of each row (transfer the stitch from the left to the right needle without working it) to create rolled edges on the underside of the strap. Felt as in step 4. Sew the strap to the top of the bag and the button to the inside of the knitting, above the lining. Use a stitch as a buttonhole.

This crocheted vase makes a lovely accessory in a natural, subtle interior. Its design is deceptively simple, but has been given a clever twist with the use of interestingly textured string.

Sisal vase

Modern crochet – in vogue again after decades in fashion wilderness – takes simple shapes in combination with contemporary colours and materials. This vase, for example, is made from none other than inexpensive garden string and uses only three different stitches. Its impact comes entirely from its pared-down profile and rough, ribbed texture. For a brighter look, you could use a combination of colours in bold stripes and, of course, you can easily adjust the pattern to make the vase as wide or narrow, tall or short as you wish.

you will need

(To make a vase measuring about 10cm diameter and 38cm high, depending on the type of string used and your tension)

- Two balls of sisal string
- 4mm crochet hook
- Scissors
- Jam jar or tin can
- Spray starch (optional)

(See page 329 for instructions on how to crochet)

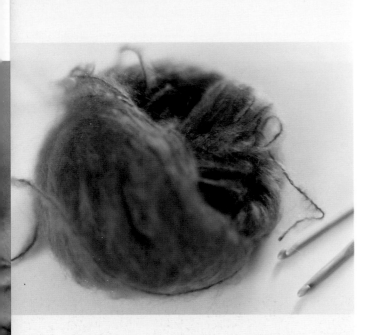

Irresistibly soft and delicate, this bed cover has a look that combines the best of classic and contemporary. While it may appear complex, the pattern can actually be built up quite simply and speedily.

Mohair throw

you will need

(To make a throw measuring about 130 x 155cm. Each motif should measure approximately 18 x 18cm. Measure the first one you make and, if it differs a great deal, you may wish to swap to a larger or smaller hook)

- 16 x 50gm balls chunky lilac pink mohair yarn (or 17 balls if you wish to use this colour for your trim)
- Two crochet hooks, sizes 5mm and 4.5mm
- 1 ball contrasting- or complementary-coloured mohair to trim (optional)

(See page 329 for instructions on how to crochet and page 77 for abbreviations)

A gorgeously soft, velvety yarn, in a fashionable colour and a pretty, feminine pattern, is what makes this project so appealing. Use two or three toning shades if you want to create a more varied look; they could be combined in stripes or blocks, or even radiate out from the centre. Finally, the beauty of the project is, of course, that you can make as many or as few squares as you wish, to create any size of cover – for a cushion or a baby's cot to a sofa or even a king-sized bed.

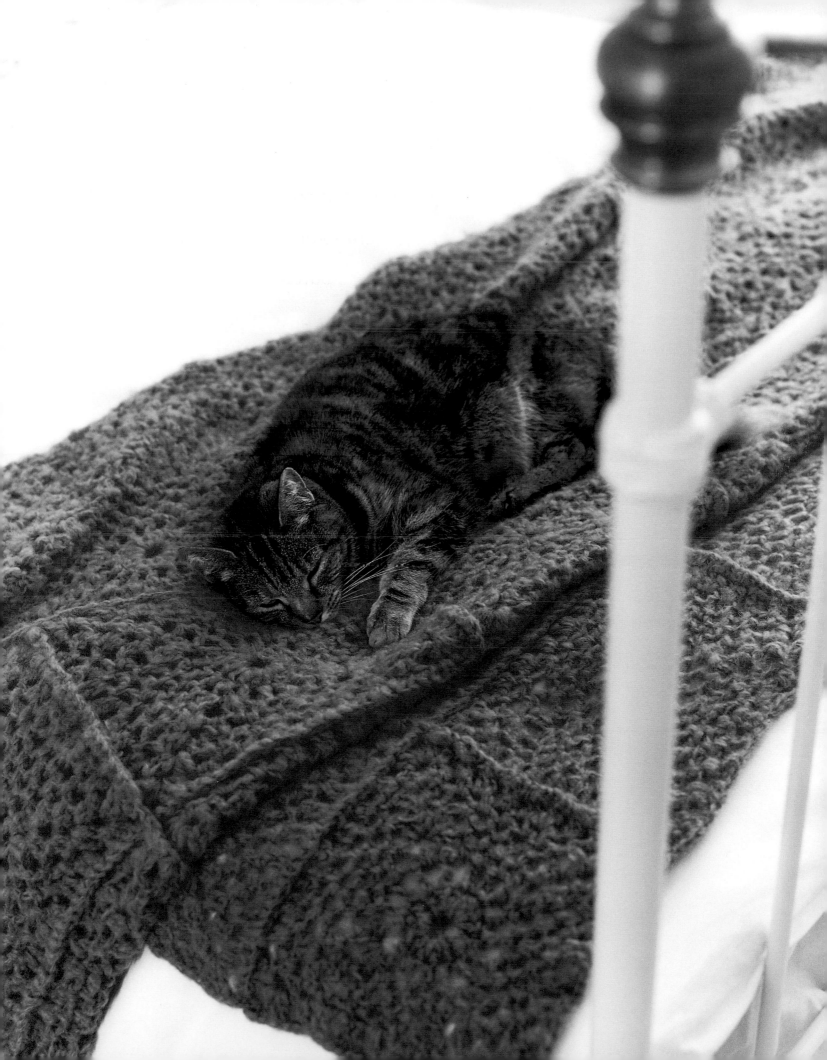

how to make: Mohair throw

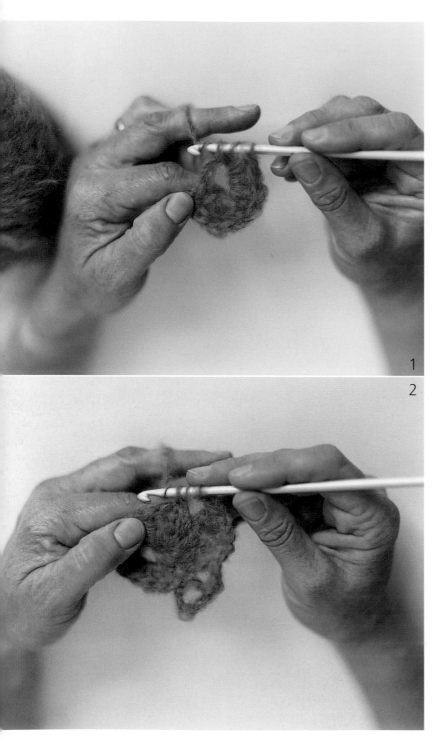

1 With the mohair yarn and the 5mm hook, make 8ch to start. Join into a ring with a sl st into the first ch, then work in rounds. Round 1: work 3ch. Work 15tr into the ring. Join with a sl st to 3rd of the 1st ch.

2 Round 2: 5ch, * 1tr into next tr, 2ch. Repeat from * 14 times then join with a sl st to 3rd of the 5ch.

3 Round 3: sl st into first space, 3ch, then 1tr, 3ch, 2tr into same space. * (2ch, 1dc into next space) 3 times. 2ch, then 2tr, 3ch, 2tr into next space. Repeat from * twice more. (2ch, 1dc into next space) 3 times. 2ch, and join with a sl st to 3rd of first 3ch. Round 4: sl st into next 3ch space, 3ch, then 1tr, 3ch, 2tr into same space.* (2ch, 1dc into 2ch space) 4 times. 2ch, then 2tr, 3ch, 2tr into 3ch space. Repeat from * twice more. (2ch, 1dc into 2ch space) 4 times. 2ch, join with a sl st to 3rd of first 3ch.

4 Round 5: as round 4, but working the repeats in brackets 5 times each. Round 6: as round 4, but working repeat in brackets 6 times. Round 7: sl st into 3ch space, 3ch, then 2tr, 2ch, 3tr into same space. * (1ch, 2tr into 2ch space) 7 times. 1ch, then 3tr, 2ch, 3tr into 3ch space. Repeat from * twice more. (1ch, 2tr into 2ch space) 5 times. 1ch, join with a sl st to 3rd of first 3ch. Fasten off by cutting the string 10cm from the hook, and drawing this 'tail' through the sl st. Trim.

5 Make enough motifs for the size of throw (this project needed 42, six motifs wide and seven long). Sew in any loose ends, then join the squares. To crochet, place two motifs together (right-sides out) and with a 5mm hook work dc through the edges of both. This gives a ridged detail. For a flatter look, stitch together.

6 With the 4.5mm hook, work one row dc around the edge of the finished throw. You may wish to do this in a contrasting or complementary colour.

3 4
5 6

Hand embroidery

The word 'embroidery' comes from the Old French *broder*, 'to decorate', and that is what it does – in one or two colours or a dazzling range of hues; with simple stitches or in an array of techniques. Embroidery embellishes, enlivens and enriches fabric using needle, thread and a vivid imagination.

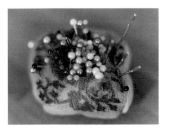

While the exact origins of decorative embroidery are rather hazy, it was certainly practised all around the world by the Middle Ages. In Europe, embroiderers formed guilds, whose workshops supplied fine vestments and hangings for the church, often under the direction of a professional painter. Belgian embroiderers, for example, were known as 'painters with the needle', and Botticelli and Durer were among those who supplied cartoons for the craft.

The most admired form of embroidery at this time was an English style known as *opus Anglicanum*. Its designs were fluid and detailed, worked in delicate stitches on a background of gold and coloured silks, often embellished with pearls and precious stones. Though some was made for aristocratic households and military purposes, it was mostly produced for ecclesiastical garments.

Religion, war, trade and social changes all played their part in the history of embroidery. In Spain, the conquering Moors set up embroidery workshops and made 'blackwork' predominant, using geometrical motifs in black and white on linen cloth. In Hungary, which was controlled by the Turks but connected with Italy, Italian threads were used with Turkish designs to create floral patterns. And when northern India was conquered by the Mongols, the second emperor brought Persian craftsmen to collaborate with the Indians.

The result was a mingling of the two styles, employing Persian motifs but naturalistic details.

After European traders reached India in the early 17th century, Indian fabrics became hugely influential in Europe. A craze developed for what was known as 'chinoiserie', where fabrics were embroidered with exotic birds, flowers and foliage, and Asian designs also inspired Jacobean crewel work, in which heavy linen was embroidered in beautifully toning woollen stitches. Today, Indian hand embroidery is still considered among the best in the world – intricate, delicate and painstakingly detailed.

In the West, 19th-century industrialization nearly put paid to embroidery as an art form. Crude synthetic dyes gave garish colours, while pre-printed canvases offered no room for creativity, and it was not until the rise of the Arts and Crafts movement, when William Morris promoted the hand-crafted over the machine-made, that embroidery came into its own again. In the second half of the 20th century the circle was completed as embroidery once again became associated with fine art. Trainee embroiderers studied life drawing and were encouraged to use stitchery as a means of artistic self-expression. Since then, hand embroidery has regained more and more respect, whether practised as an art form or simply an enjoyable means of relaxation, and whether pushing back the boundaries in terms of new concepts and experimentation, or reinforcing its rich history by using the traditional techniques of the past.

This napkin is so pretty, it's almost a shame to use it! The charming motif of a fantastical flower combines whimsy and daintiness to enliven an otherwise classic table setting.

Flower napkins

(To make six napkins, each 41cm square)
- Six pieces of natural linen, each measuring 41cm square
- Sewing machine
- Cotton thread to match the linen
- Scissors
- Pencil
- Tracing paper
- Dressmaker's carbon paper
- Masking tape
- 20cm diameter embroidery hoop
- Size three embroidery needle
- 1 skein each of cotton embroidery thread in red, pink, pale pink, lilac, pale blue, dark green, pale yellow and bright green
- Iron

Traditional embroiderers may find that this project strays too far from the usual realm of tiny stitches and straightforward motifs. What this project does, however, is to show how a combination of time-honoured hand embroidery stitches can be interpreted in a way that is thoroughly modern, yet still highly appealing. The colours shown here are soft and pretty, though it would also be interesting to use vivid shades for a bold, bright look. The attractive fringed edging is a thoughtful touch that complements the napkin's lively informality.

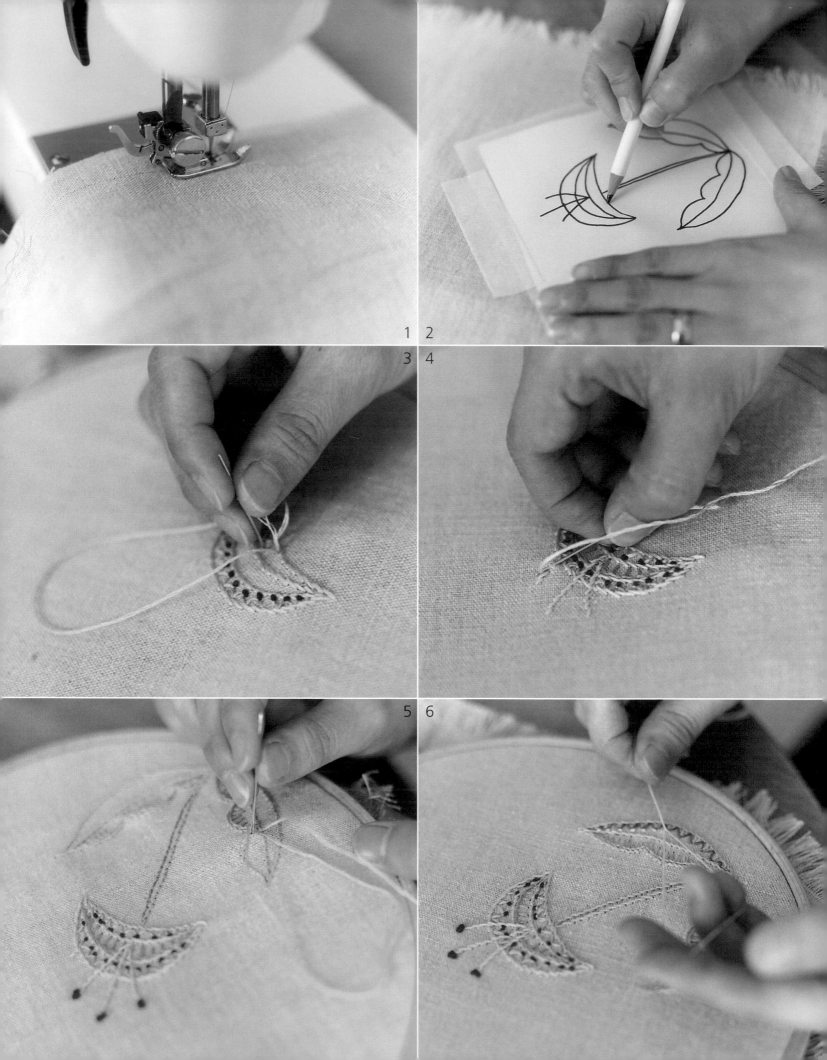

how to make:
Flower napkins

7

8

stitches used
Fly stitch, blanket stitch, stem stitch, double cross stitch, knot.

1 Take the linen squares and use the sewing machine to stitch a line all the way round, 1.5cm in from the edges of the cloth, following the warp and weft as much as possible. Fray the edges of the fabric almost up to the stitching.

2 Trace the design on page 327 onto a piece of tracing paper. Lay this over a piece of dressmaker's carbon paper and tape both of them onto the fabric, so that the design is in one corner. Draw over the design. As an alternative, you could draw out your own pattern. Experiment on a piece of paper first.

3 Remove the paper and sandwich the fabric into the embroidery hoop. Start to embroider the design, using three strands of thread for all colours. Begin with the flower head, and stem stitch along the outer and middle lines to define its shape. On the inside of this line, fly stitch to create definition, adding a knot at the end of each fly stitch.

4 Between the two middle lines at the centre of the flower, stitch a line of blanket stitches. The stamens are made by three lines of stem stitch, each finished with a knot (use six strands of thread for these knots).

5 Create the stalk by sewing two parallel lines of stem stitch, then two leaves and a central vein, also in stem stitch. Oversew a line of blanket stitch along the leading edge of both leaves to create definition.

6 Sew a line of fly stitches along the inside of the bottom edge of the leaves. In the centre of each fly stitch make one short stitch and finish each stitch with a knot.

7 To finish off, embroider a double cross stitch and a knot in all four corners of the napkin, plus a single knot in between.

8 Press carefully with a warm iron on the wrong side of the napkin, to ensure that you do not damage the finished embroidery.

stitches used

VVVVV	fly stitch	||||||| satin stitch
ΠΠΠΠ	blanket stitch	
⁓⁓⁓⁓	stem stitch	chain stitch
X	cross stitch	
✳	double cross stitch	basket stitch
⊘	knot	

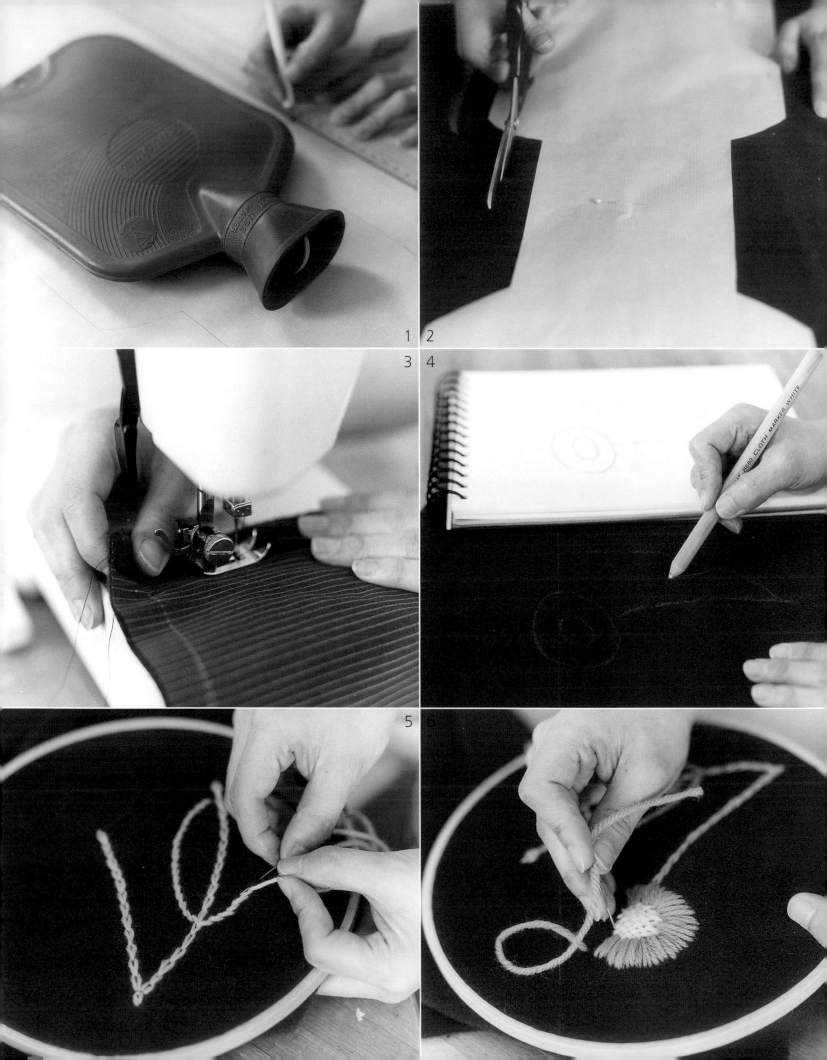

how to make:
Hot water bottle cover

stitches used

Chain stitch, stem stitch, basket stitch, cross stitch, satin stitch, knot (see page 87 for illustrations).

1 Place the hot water bottle on a large sheet of paper. Draw around it, but make the bottom 5cm shorter. Flip the bottle over at the neck and draw around it again, but this time extending its length by one third (see page 327). Allowing an extra 2cm all round, cut out.

2 Pin the paper pattern to the fleece and draw a line around it with the tailor's chalk pencil. Cut out, allowing an extra 2cm all round. Repeat with the cotton (this will act as a lining and help the fleece keep shape).

3 Sew a 1cm hem on the top and bottom edges of both the fleece and the cotton. Press.

4 Tack the fleece to the cotton, wrong sides together (you will embroider through both layers). Using the tailor's chalk pencil, copy the design on page 327 onto the fleece in the position shown.

5 Sandwich the fabric into the embroidery hoop. Begin to embroider the design. Start with a single line of chain stitch to create the stem and the stalk of the leaf. Next, sew a line of stem stitch to make the leaf itself. Chain stitch three separate lines to define the veins of the leaf. Make a knot at the end of each vein.

6 At the top of the flower stem, basket stitch the centre of the flower head. Create the surrounding petals by sewing satin stitches.

7 Sew flower stamens using a series of knots all over the basket stitch area. Scatter a few cross stitches with a centre knot around the rest of the cover to finish.

8 Fold the fabric, right sides together, at the neck, and then fold over the flap at the bottom too, as shown by the dotted lines in the diagram on page 327. Machine stitch both side seams, following the chalk line you drew in step 2 (this gives a 2cm seam allowance), and clip any curves. Turn out and press.

7

8

protecting the fabric

To prevent the embroidery hoop from marking the fleece, always remove the fabric at the end of each sewing session.

cutting thread

When sewing, cut each length of thread to about 25cm – any longer and it will be difficult to work with.

how to make: **Lavender pouch**

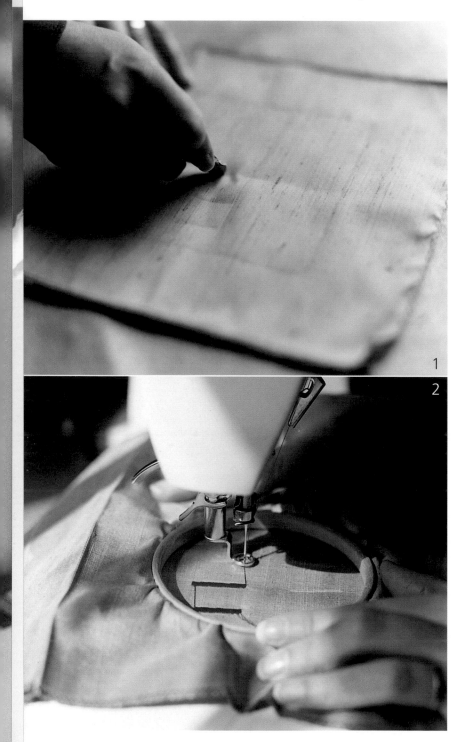

1

2

1 Zig-zag the edges of your fabric. Fold in half and iron. On one side of the folded fabric, mark a rectangle for the lavender – about 4cm in from the folded edge and 5cm in from the zig-zag edges. Use the embroidery pen to draw ten horizontal lines at regular intervals in the centre of this.

2 For this stage, it is possible to use an ordinary sewing machine, but the finished result may be neater if you use an embroidery machine and hoop. Embroider the design, creating a satin stitch by zig-zagging very close together about 0.5cm long. The hoop will have to be moved across in order to complete the design. For an irregular effect, you can change the width of the stitch with each line you sew. Press on the wrong side to make the embroidery stand out.

3 Fold the fabric in half, this time with the good embroidery side in, and stitch the side seams with a 1cm seam allowance, leaving one end open.

4 Turn out and, with the right side of the embroidery facing you, stitch along three sides of the rectangle marked in step 1, leaving the same side open as in step 3.

5 Pour the lavender into the small rectangle and pin it closed. Stitch neatly along the remaining line.

6 Turn in 1cm of the remaining open side and iron to make a neat edge. Stitch together, keeping the stitching as close to the edge as you can.

filling the pouch
Be careful not to overfill the pouch with lavender or it will be difficult to stitch closed.

variations
If you want to experiment with the stitching, you could create your own design using continuous zig-zag lines in toning shades of more than one colour.

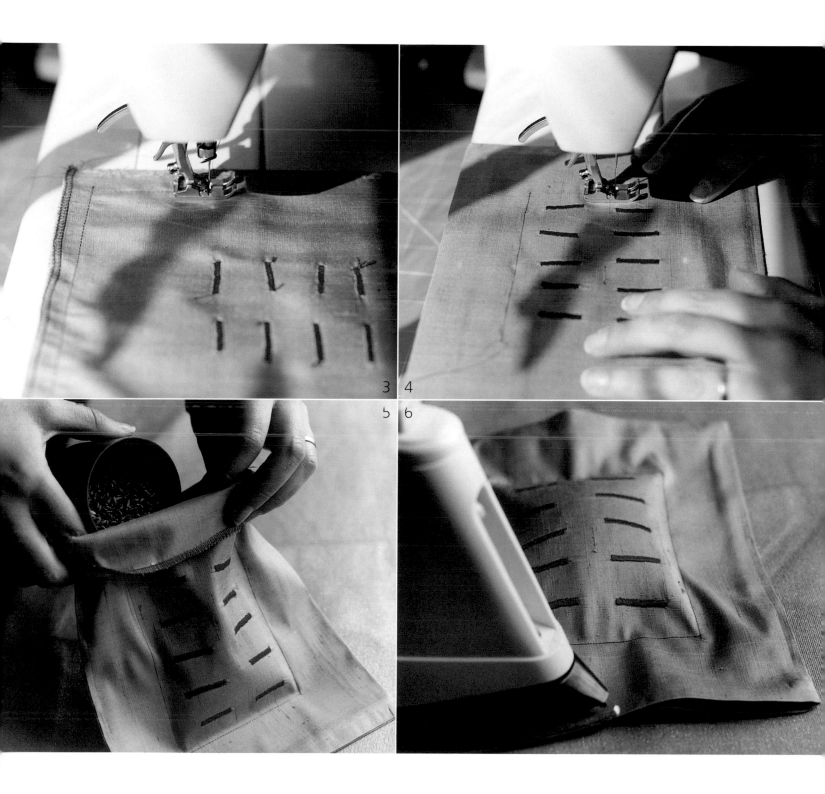

3 4

5 6

The elegant beauty of this classic design just never seems to date. Ivory lettering on an unbleached linen background is chic and simple for either town or country.

Laundry bag

you will need

(To make a bag measuring 52 x 72cm)

- 2m oyster-white linen, at least 110cm wide
- Ruler
- Scissors
- Iron
- Sewing machine, preferably with the facility to do freehand embroidery (a freehand embroidery foot is helpful, too, though not essential)
- Satin-finish synthetic thread to match the fabric
- Safety pin
- 'Invisible' embroidery pen or pale-coloured tailor's chalk
- 20cm diameter machine embroidery hoop
- Pins

Anyone who has ever been even vaguely interested in the art of calligraphy will appreciate the subtle beauty of pared-down, flowing lettering. This project borrows a little from that craft and translates it into another – machine embroidery – and substitutes fabric for paper, thread for ink. The result is truly lovely, taking an old-fashioned drawstring bag design in plain, soft linen, and combining it with loose, modern stitchcraft to transform a very functional object into something that is an absolute joy to use.

how to make: Laundry bag

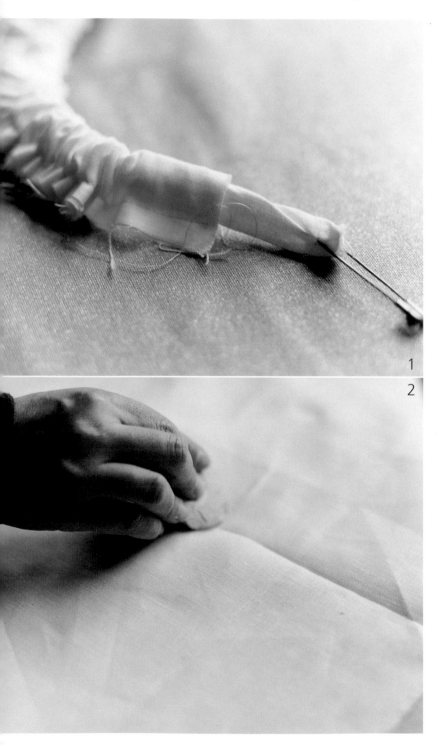

1

2

1 To make the drawstring, cut a rectangle of linen 6cm x 2m. Fold it right sides together along the length and press. Stitch along, leaving 1cm seam allowance, then turn out, using a safety pin. Press again. Tuck the ends into the tube and stitch across neatly to secure them.

2 Cut out two rectangles of linen each 52 x 85cm and zig-zag along the raw edges. Using the ruler and embroidery pen or tailor's chalk, mark a horizontal line on the right side of one of the rectangles, about 15cm up from the bottom edge. This indicates the positioning of the centre of your lettering. Test how long the word will be by practising on a piece of spare fabric, then mark three dots on the line for the first letter, the middle and the end. (If you wish, you can write out the whole word, though if you embroider freely you will create a looser, 'handwriting' style.)

3 Sandwich the fabric, with the marked embroidery area visible, into the embroidery hoop so that it is as taut as possible. Carefully embroider your letters, creating a satin stitch by zig-zagging about 0.5cm long and very close together. Remove the fabric from the hoop. Iron on the back of the embroidery to make the letters stand out.

4 Pin the two large pieces of fabric together with the right (embroidered) side in. Stitch three sides (with 1cm seam allowance), leaving the top open.

5 Keeping the bag inside out, turn the top edge out 12cm. Iron, then mark two horizontal lines around the bag, 5cm and 8cm from the top edge – this is for the drawstring. Stitch along both lines. When you stitch over the side seams, go back and forth a few times to fasten the stitches beneath securely. Turn the bag the right way round and, on the right-hand side seam, unpick the 3cm of stitching between the two rows you have just stitched.

6 Attach a safety pin to your drawstring, and pull it through the gap between the two stitched lines. Gather and tie in a bow.

3 4
5 6

Cosy and comfortable, this bed cover takes a classic design and updates it with modern fabric. A perfect blend of old and new, its look is chic, clean and sophisticated. It could happily grace a bedroom of any style.

Bed cover

you will need

(To make a bed cover measuring 1 x 2m)

- Tailor's chalk
- Ruler
- 2.1m cornflower blue silk satin (must be at least 1m wide) for the top of the quilt
- Pins
- 2.1m silk satin to match the top silk satin (or cotton; must be at least 1m wide) for the bottom of the quilt
- Sewing machine with a fine 70s needle
- Thread to match the top colour fabric
- Scissors
- Iron
- 2.5m of 12oz wadding (90cm wide)
- Sewing needle
- Long, fine quilting needle

Although quilted satin bed covers are the height of contemporary fashion, this version employs stobbed quilting, one of the craft's oldest forms. Quick and highly effective, it simply involves knotting the layers together with a small stitch at regular intervals. For variety, you may wish to make the reverse side from a patterned fabric (perhaps to coordinate with your décor). Or use thinner wadding and machine stitch a decorative pattern – criss-cross lines, in a square or diamond pattern, for example, would be a pleasantly subtle, modern interpretation of the theme.

how to make: **Bed cover**

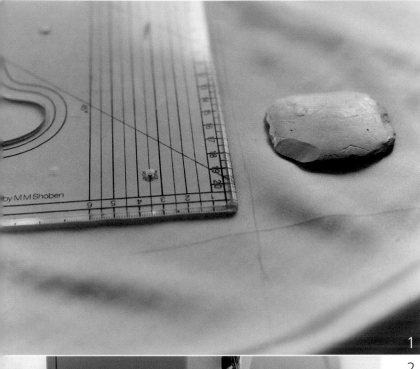

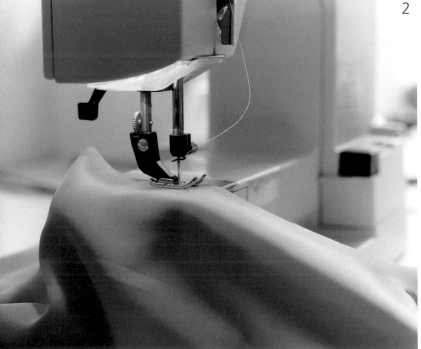

1. With the chalk, lightly draw a pinpoint grid in a criss-cross design on the right side of the fabric that you have chosen for the top of the quilt.

2. Pin this fabric to the bottom fabric, with the right sides together. Stitch around the sides, allowing 1.5cm seam allowance and being careful not to pucker the fabric. Leave a 70cm gap on one of the short sides.

3. Cut the corners at a 45 degree angle. Turn out, then press, so that the seam is crisp and straight.

4. Insert the wadding, ensuring it is flat and fits properly into the corners. Hand stitch the opening neatly.

5. Pin at the chalk dots, checking that both the front and back of the fabric are smooth. With a long quilting needle threaded double, hand-stitch the three layers of fabric and wadding together at one of the pinned points. Stab stitch several times, pulling the stitches as firmly as possible to ensure a luxurious padded effect.

6. Tie off each thread neatly and securely on the reverse side of the quilt. Repeat at each of the pinned points.

variations

If you prefer, you can use a lighter weight wadding and neatly machine stitch lines in a square or diamond pattern over your bed cover.

If you want to make a double bed cover, simply double the width of both fabric and wadding – if the wadding isn't wide enough, hand-sew two widths together first.

3 4
5 6

This wrap is warm and comforting yet surprisingly light and delicate. The graphic ombré silk combines with the abstract stitched pattern for a contemporary take on traditional quilting.

Ombré wrap

you will need

(To make a wrap measuring 38 x 144cm)

- Iron
- 40 x 160cm lightweight iron-on interfacing
- Enough ombré silk to cut two pieces, measuring 40 x 160cm and 40 x 146cm, both with a good variety of shading (this project used shades of grey)
- Scissors
- Measuring tape
- Tailor's chalk
- Pins
- Sewing machine
- Thread to match the silk
- 40 x 146cm thin interlining
- Needle

This wrap has been designed with energetic lines of stitching contained within pieced sections of ombré silk, the juxtaposition of discipline and free-flowing lines making for a highly appealing composition. Simple to make, the project can be easily adapted to other sizes and colours, or even other fabrics – though the silk ombré is a particularly striking choice, and feels very luxurious next to the skin. In this muted shade it is easy to wear, and would look as good with a smart business suit as with an elegant evening dress.

how to make:
Ombré wrap

1 Iron the interfacing to the wrong side of the
40 x 160cm silk rectangle. Cut this piece into eight
rectangles of 20 x 40cm. On a large work surface or
the floor, re-arrange the pieces into one big rectangle,
but this time with the shading directions alternating.

2 With the chalk, lightly draw a design of curving lines
onto the right side of each section. With right sides
together, pin then stitch the rectangles together, allowing
1cm seam allowance, and press the seams flat.

3 Lay the interlining flat on your work surface, and place
the second piece of silk on top of it, right side up. Place
the stitched silk on top, right side down. Pin together, then
machine stitch around all four sides, allowing a 1cm seam
allowance, but leaving a gap the width of one stitched
section. Turn out, press, and hand-stitch the opening.

4 Pin along the seam lines, working from the centre
outwards, checking that both front and back are
smooth. This will section off each area and make the piece
more workable. Machine stitch along each seam line,
through all three layers, to start to create a padded effect.

5 Pin along one of the chalk lines you drew in step 2,
again working from the centre outwards to avoid
puckering and checking that both front and back are
smooth. Stitch through all three layers. Pin and stitch all
the lines, changing the bobbin and top thread occasionally,
to match roughly the changing shading on the top layer of
ombré. Hold down the fabric and manoeuvre the quilt
under the needle, taking care to regulate both stitch length
and straightness. Remember that if you have drawn any
tight curves you will have to remove the presser foot from
the sewing machine, lower the teeth and the presser foot
lever, and free machine embroider.

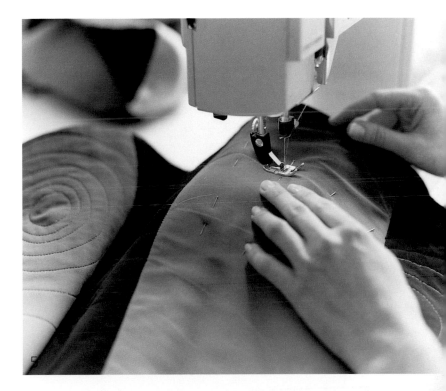

neat stitching
Make sure that the spiral machine stitching is as neat
and fluid as possible, by keeping the action continuous
and turning the fabric cleanly as you go. The finished
effect will be tidy and professional-looking.

Appliqué

What better way to make the most of worn-out or leftover fabric than to turn it into another, perhaps more beautiful, textile? Appliqué does just that – its use is as old as cloth itself and its designs as varied as the different societies, ancient and modern, that have discovered its decorative power.

Whether for repair or decoration, the use of scraps of one fabric stitched on (or applied to) another is common to most cultures and probably stretches back to the very first items of clothing. The Eskimos of northern Alaska, for example, made coats from appliquéd skins, adorned with stitches and beadwork, while North American Indians made appliqué from birch bark sewn with spruce roots; the peasants of Persia created felt-work appliqué in bold designs, while leather appliqué in bright colours and intricate floral designs is typical of Hungary.

One of the oldest forms of appliqué is the *suradeq*, an Egyptian tent lined with exquisite, hand-stitched appliquéd forms in red, black, yellow, green and blue. Their patterns are based on ancient Pharonic art and Coptic and Islamic motifs, including lotus flowers, geometric shapes and calligraphy. The tents are made by men only, in designs passed down from generation to generation. Centuries ago, Egyptian rulers used the suradeq as travelling palaces, transporting them across the deserts on camels, and today new tents are still made for special celebrations.

In Central America, the women of the Cuna tribe, of the San Blas Islands in Panama, still make colourful *molas*, or blouses, from appliquéd cloth. Newer versions employ standard appliqué, embellished with decorative stitching, but traditional molas use complex reverse appliqué, where pieces of fabric are stitched together in layers, then patterns cut from them and hemmed back to reveal the colours beneath. The best examples are collectors' pieces, highly prized as works of art.

Examples of European appliqué made for the aristocracy can be found as far back as the Middle Ages. It was rich and colourful, used for wall hangings (the only way to keep out draughts in a medieval manor), clothing, clerical vestments and heraldry. It was also a good substitute for expensive solid embroidery and whole brocades or velvets. And, from the late-18th century, appliqué was used to make quilt covers; the American settlers went on to develop this as a widely practised domestic art form – thrifty, inventive and extraordinarily skilful.

Appliqué came to the fore again in late-19th-century Britain, thanks to the proponents of the Arts and Crafts school, who urged a return to well-crafted, hand-made things. Appliqué was seen as particularly appropriate to their aesthetic, and emphasis was placed on stylized designs and simple fabrics such as hessian and satin, rather than expensive cloth and intricate stitching. Such thinking has remained predominant today, as craftspeople working with appliqué continue to explore its versatility. It can be abstract or figurative, as simple or as complex as the maker desires, in plain or unexpected cloth, embellished with additional stitching or left for the fabrics to speak for themselves – a spontaneous craft that crosses all barriers.

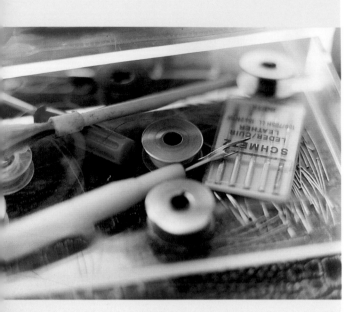

The striking simplicity of this appliquéd placemat is its strongest feature – a spare motif, two colours and some careful stitching make it an arresting home accessory.

Leaf tablemats

you will need

(To make six tablemats, 38.5 x 48.5cm)
- Six pieces of pale blue/grey linen, each measuring 40 x 50cm
- Pins
- Iron
- Sewing machine
- Cotton thread to either match or contrast with the two colours of linen
- Scissors
- Small piece of green linen
- Beading, or very fine, needle
- 30 seed beads in a variety of coordinating colours

A pattern of curving leaves lends itself beautifully to this straightforward project, though as you become more skilled in the art of appliqué you may wish to develop the design to incorporate more complex shapes, and maybe even further colours, too. Texture and colour are very important here, and the delicately woven surface of the linen works with the appliquéd cut-outs and the tracery of stitching to create subtle interest. The beaded edging finishes things off with decorative flair.

how to make:
Leaf tablemats

1 Turn a narrow double hem along all sides of each linen rectangle, taking care that the corners are neat. Pin and press. Stitch the hem in either a complementary or contrasting colour.

2 Cut a stem and leaves from the green linen (see diagram on page 325). Snip small cuts, about 0.5cm long, around the edges of the leaves.

3 Turn the edges of the leaves under and arrange in place, around the stem, on the tablemat. Pin, then press.

4 Straight stitch neatly down the middle of the stem, using either a complementary- or contrasting-colour thread. Remove the pins as you go.

5 Then, straight stitch neatly around the edges of the leaves, as close to the edges as possible, again removing the pins as you go. Press the tablemat on the wrong side.

6 To finish, sew the beads, about 3cm apart, along the short edges of the tablemat, using one continuous thread hidden in the hem.

turning a double hem
To turn a double hem, simply fold over the edge of the fabric and press, then fold over again, pin, press and stitch.

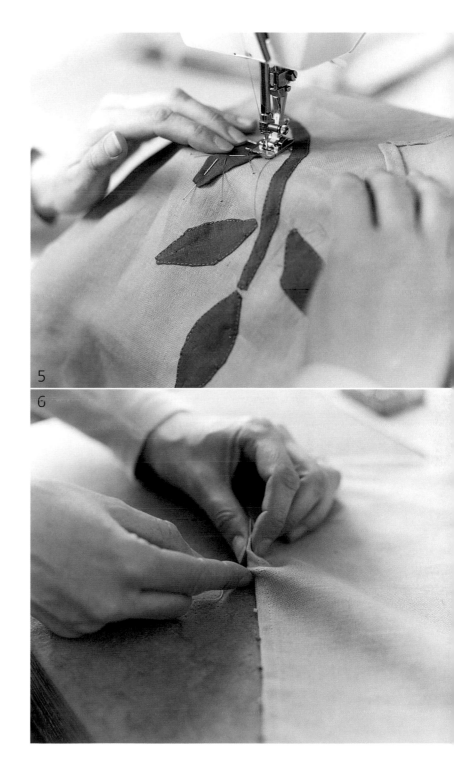

5

6

For a charming and stylish table setting, this appliquéd cloth is ideal. Although striking, it is understated enough to be a perfect complement to crockery, cutlery and glassware.

Kitchen tablecloth

you will need

(To make a tablecloth measuring about 154cm square)

- Four pieces of coordinating linen, each cut to 78cm square (this project uses lemon yellow, soft pink, grey/blue and soft turquoise/blue
- Pins
- Sewing machine
- Cotton threads to complement and contrast with the colours of linen
- Scissors
- Scraps of different-coloured linen
- Iron
- Needle

What makes this tablecloth special is the clever repetition of colour and pattern, with motifs placed carefully in an apparently random pattern. Choose any colours you wish and experiment with different cut-out shapes (but keep them simple) and decorative overstitching. The size of the cloth can, of course, be varied according to your table. It could also be extremely effective to make matching place mats that feature coordinating colours and designs; or to use this technique to create a set of cushions or napkins, or even a unique wall hanging.

how to make: **Kitchen tablecloth**

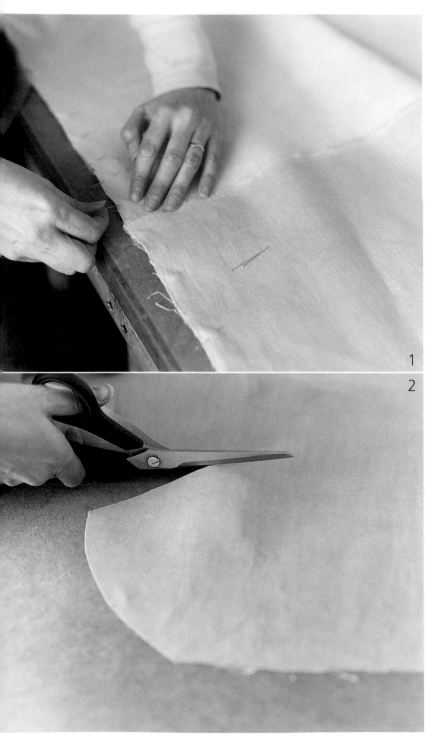

1

2

1 First, stitch the four linen squares together to make one large square. Pin two pieces right sides together and stitch one edge, allowing 0.5cm seam allowance. Zig-zag the raw edges to prevent fraying and press flat, pushing the seam to one side. Repeat with the other two pieces, then stitch the two larger pieces together in the same way. On the right side of the fabric, sew over the two seams, so the stitches show on the top of the tablecloth.

2 Cut the bowl, cups and leaves motifs from the different-coloured scraps of linen (see diagram on page 325). Snip small cuts, about 0.5cm long, around the edges of the curves.

3 Turn the edges of the motifs under and arrange in place on the tablecloth. Check the composition by standing well back. Pin, then press carefully.

4 Straight stitch neatly around the edges of the motifs, as close to the edges as possible, using either complementary- or contrasting-coloured threads. Remove the pins as you go. Press.

5 Add lines of tiny hand stitching to emphasize the lines on the cups and bowls, using complementary-coloured thread.

6 Turn a narrow double hem all around the tablecloth, pin and then press. To finish, stitch the hem in either a complementary or contrasting colour.

variations
You may wish to use other shapes of your own design to decorate your tablecloth. If so, keep the shapes as simple as possible. Make sure, too, that your designs are not too large, or they may overwhelm and give the tablecloth an imbalanced feel.

3 4
5 6

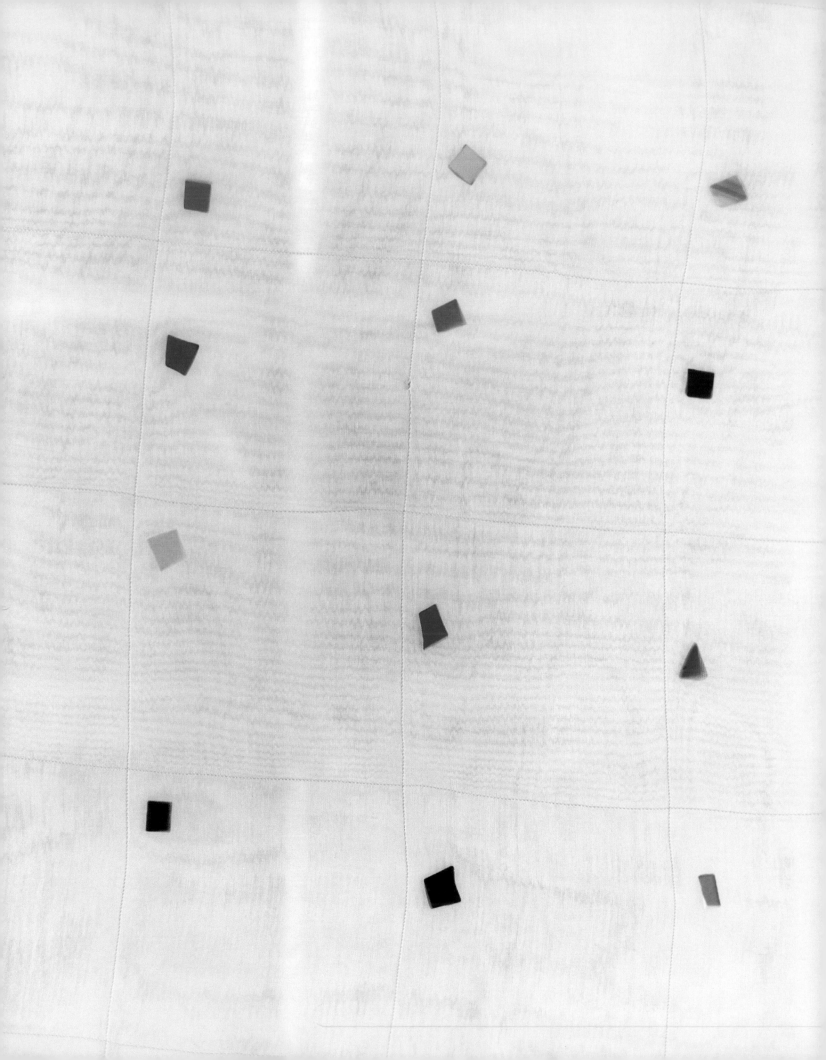

Complex textiles

For thousands of years we have embellished textiles in a variety of ways, from dyeing and painting to stitching and ribbonwork. Each technique can be used on its own, but the most dazzling results come about when they are combined, using modern techniques and materials to create a complex and impressive effect.

Once man had learnt how to spin yarn and weave cloth, he soon developed ways of embellishing the fabric to make it even more decorative and desirable. Textile dyes were used in China well over 4,000 years ago, and by the Middle Ages the Japanese were combining sophisticated dyeing techniques with intricate hand embroidery and free brushwork to create gorgeous kimonos with complex surface patterns. In Medieval Europe, meanwhile, stitchery was a highly accomplished craft, and appliqué and embroidery were used together in fabulous wall hangings, clothing, clerical vestments and heraldry. From the late-18th century onwards, appliqué and stitching were combined in quilted bed covers, which were made with extraordinarily high levels of skill in both Britain and America.

Quilting is now undergoing something of a revival, as are appliqué, beading and embroidery. In fact, a wide range of traditional textile techniques have been brought back to life in the last few decades, treasured for what previously made them unfashionable – the fact that they are time-consuming, more expensive than their machine-made counterparts and require meticulous attention to detail. When used together, these techniques are highly effective; when used in conjunction with cutting-edge techniques and materials, they can be truly stunning.

A contemporary branch of textile art that has sprung up only in the last decade is a fascination with the layering of sheer fabrics and the effects that can be achieved by combining those layers with other types of fabric, with dyed areas of cloth, with stitching and with three-dimensional objects trapped between the layers. One reason for this must be the new trend in simple, streamlined fashion and home decoration, where texture has overtaken colour as a predominant consideration; another is the ease with which modern sewing machines can create all sorts of intricate effects easily and quickly.

Yet another is the ready availability of all sorts of intriguing new fabrics, man-made or natural, which offer the textile designer endless possibilities for experimentation. New forms of dye, too, give the craftsperson a host of innovative methods to try – not forgetting natural dyes, which have also experienced a renaissance in recent years. And, finally, there is the impetus of exploring and remembering the past through today's eyes, which is seen in the cycles of retro-chic fashion and in the work of craftspeople whose aim is to create a 21st century heirloom. By suspending beads, glass, pebbles or small mementos within delicately stitched pockets of fabric, made into wall hangings, pictures, cushions, bags, throws and even dresses, it is possible to capture memories, to stimulate the senses and to embody a variety of age-old techniques in a way that could not be more new and exciting.

While primarily a decorative object – perfect for a bedroom, bathroom, hallway or even kitchen – this hanging tidy would also be useful for storing and displaying small, light, delicate items.

Hanging tidy

you will need

(To make a tidy measuring 60 x 75cm)
- White cotton organdie, measuring 105 x 120cm
- Scissors
- Ruler
- Pins
- 6m white cotton bias binding
- Sewing machine
- White thread
- 'Invisible' embroidery pen
- Decorative inserts (such as buttons, small shells, glass beads or flat pebbles)
- Iron
- Pale green cold-water dye (optional)

The sewing techniques necessary to make this tidy, with its rows of different-sized pockets, are pretty straightforward. The project's clever touch is in its incorporation of tiny inserts that are trapped between the thin layers of organdie to provide shadowy decoration. The choice of objects to enclose is all part of the enjoyment, as is the selection of a pretty rod – be it bamboo, wood, slender wrought iron or shiny stainless steel – from which to hang the tidy.

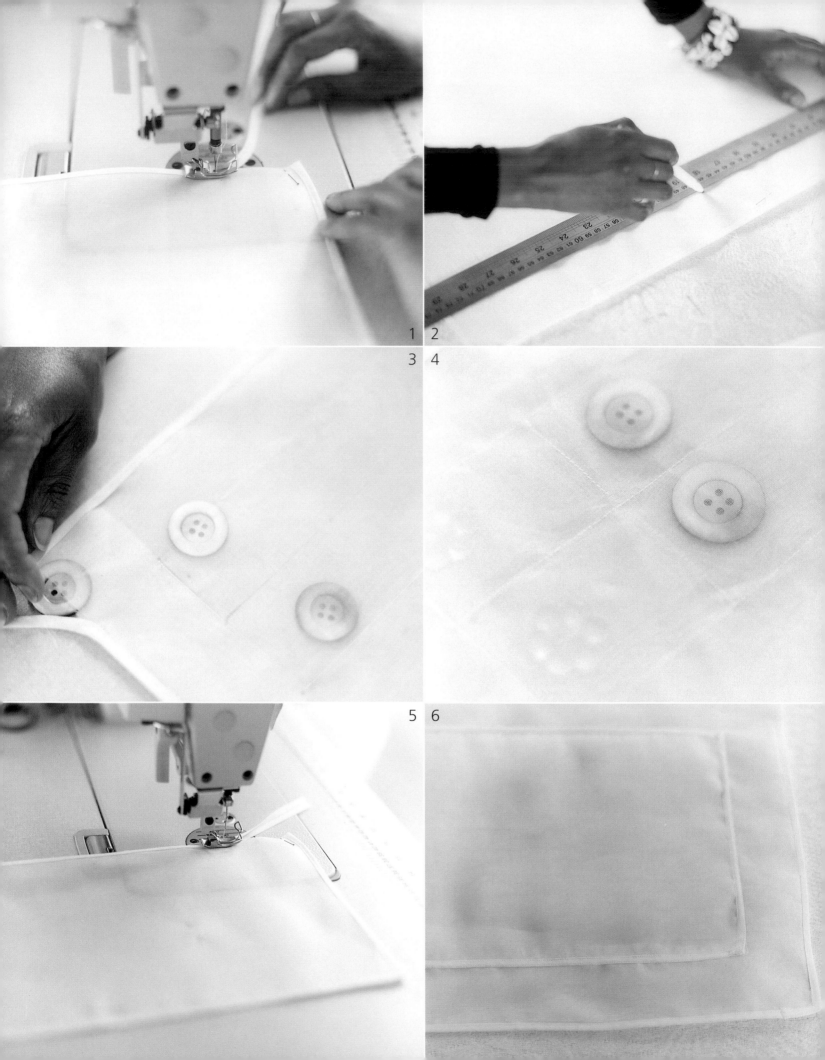

how to make:
Hanging tidy

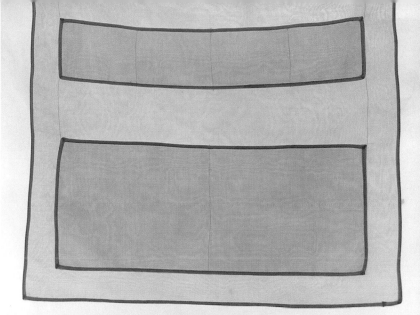

1 Fold your fabric in half lengthways and cut out two each of the following rectangles: 60 x 75cm (A), 20 x 50cm (B) and 10 x 50cm (C). Pin the two layers of shape A together, wrong sides facing, and edge with bias binding, leaving a gap in the top edge large enough to slip your inserts in.

2 Using the embroidery pen, draw a 5cm-deep border inside the bias binding, and stitch along this line, leaving a gap opposite the one in the bias binding of the same size.

3 Stitch another line, 10cm below the top border line, and push the inserts in. Divide them in half, and stitch another line between them, 5cm below the top border line.

4 Stitch the two gaps closed. Separate the inserts into pairs by stitching vertically across the enclosure.

5 Take shape B and pin the layers together securely, with the wrong sides facing. Edge with bias binding. Repeat with shape C.

6 Take shape B and place it across the bottom of the border in shape A. Stretch it flat and pin. Attach with two lines of stitching (on the outer and inner edges of the bias binding) along both sides and the bottom.

7 Repeat step 6 with shape C, placing it about 10cm above the top of shape B. Mark a vertical line at the mid point of each pocket and stitch along, creating two pockets in each. Mark two further vertical lines at the mid points of the two pockets in shape C and stitch along them, creating four pockets. Press, avoiding the inserts.

8 Take 50cm of bias binding and stitch the edges together to form a long tape. Cut into five equal portions and fold in half to form loops. Mark points at 15cm intervals on the reverse side of the tidy at the top edge. Sew a tape to each point. If you wish, you can dye the finished tidy with cold-water dye, following the manufacturer's instructions.

7

8

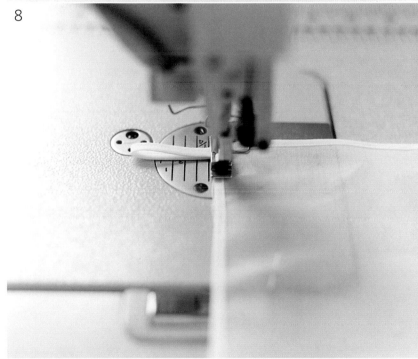

working with bias binding
When edging the fabric with bias binding, it is helpful to crease the binding in half along its length first, then stitch along both the right and the wrong sides to ensure that it is attached firmly.

The frothy layers of this organdie are utterly delightful, and here they are brought into clever contrast with the solidity of a dyed motif and a variety of tiny trapped objects.

Flower cushion

you will need

(To make a cushion measuring about 35 x 35cm)

- 2m white cotton organdie (at least 102cm wide)
- Ruler
- Scissors
- Pins
- Iron
- 'Invisible' embroidery pen
- 2.7m length of 1.5cm-wide white cotton bias binding
- Sewing machine
- White thread
- Plate (about 25cm diameter) or pair of compasses
- Masking tape
- Bowl or box
- Paintbrush
- Small bottle blue silk paint or dye
- Decorative inserts (such as small glass buttons, shells or flat pebbles)
- White 35cm square cushion pad
- Cold-water dye (optional)

This project is relatively complicated as it contains a number of different processes – from cutting and stitching to layering and entrapment – but it is the combination of these various techniques that gives the finished cushion its precise sophistication and professional appearance. Take it slowly and carefully and you shouldn't run into any problems. In white, the cushion has a cloudy, ethereal look. You could easily, however, dye the fabric any colour of your choice, or vary the colour of the painted motif.

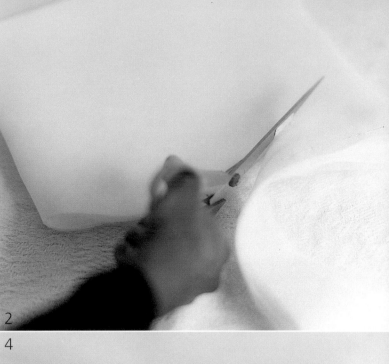

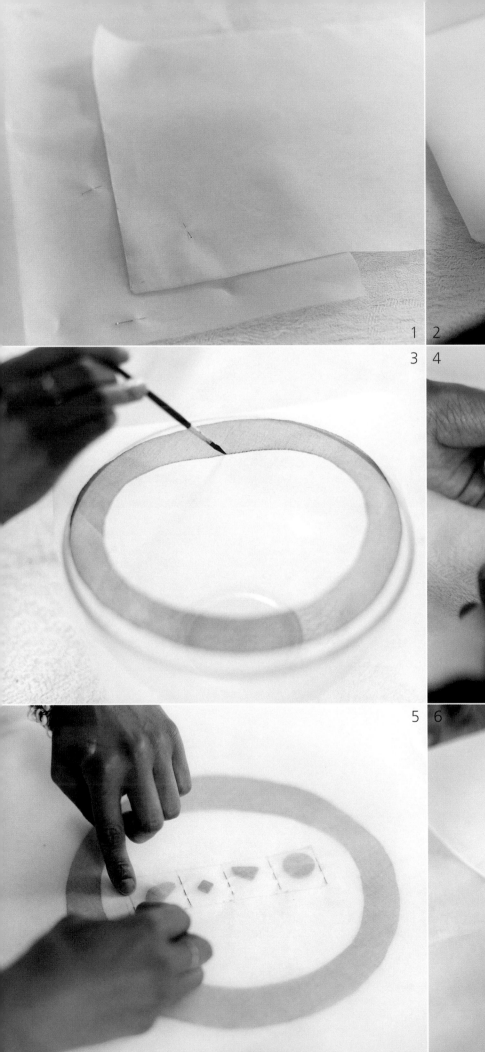

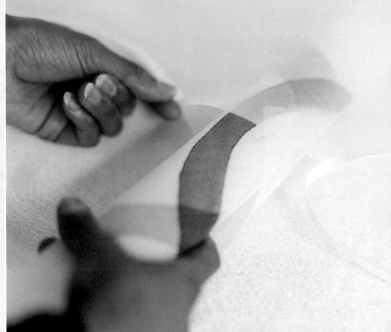

how to make:
Flower cushion

1 Take the organdie and cut out two shapes 60 x 60cm and pin securely, wrong sides together (A). Cut a square 40 x 40cm (B). Cut two rectangles 42 x 82cm and pin securely, right sides together (C). Press them with a hot iron.

2 Fold shape A into a flat quarter. With the embroidery pen, draw the shape of a petal (see template on page 324) ensuring that the starting and finishing points have the same depth. Cut along this line through the layers of fabric. Unfold and remove enough pins to iron flat. Edge with bias binding, leaving a 10cm gap for the inserts. Remove the pins.

3 Take square B and draw a circle with a diameter of around 25cm in the centre of the fabric, either around a plate or using a pair of compasses. Handling the fabric gently so as not to distort its shape, tape the corners onto a bowl or box to give you a flat surface on which to paint. Lightly paint around the edge of the circle with the silk dye, creating an irregularly shaped line about 3 or 4cm wide.

4 When the dye is dry, iron the fabric to fix it (follow manufacturer's instructions). The fabric does not need hemming, but you can fray the edges for decorative effect. Roll the fabric into a sausage shape and insert it into the gap left in shape A. Unroll using a ruler and ease into the centre of the flower shape. Iron flat and pin into position.

5 With the embroidery pen, draw the shape in which the inserts will be positioned. Insert them into the cushion cover above the painted shape B. Pin into position, then sew around them (through all the layers) to secure in place.

6 Stretch and fold a 30cm length of bias binding and stitch the outside edges together to form a tape. Cut into two equal lengths. Attach one end of one of these lengths to the wrong side of A/B in the centre, at the top of the design. Take shape C (the two rectangles you pinned together in step 1) and stitch around the edge of the rectangle 1cm in, leaving about 10cm unstitched. Ensure that the edge outside the stitching is neat; trim if necessary. Remove pins and turn out carefully. Press flat.

7 Make the cushion flap. Fold C in half lengthways and mark the halfway point at top and bottom. Unfold and lightly draw a line joining the halfway points. Overstitch around one half of the fabric, along the line and around the

7
8

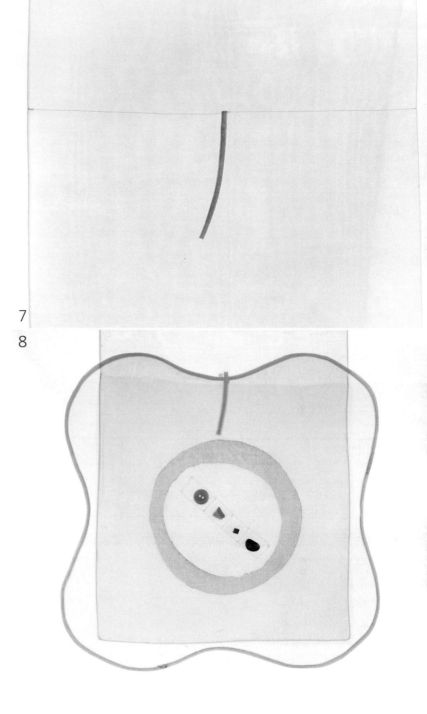

three remaining edges (see diagram on page 324), as close to the edge as possible. Attach one end of the second piece of tape to the centre of the fabric, lying it in the stitched half.

8 Take shape A/B and place it right side facing down. Place C on top, right-side up, with the unstitched half of shape C over A/B, aligning it with B. Make sure both tapes align at the top of the cushion. Pin A/B and C together and stitch along three sides of the unstitched half of C, as close to the edge as possible. Remove all pins and insert the cushion pad, tucking down the flap of C smoothly inside the sleeve. Tie the tapes. If you wish, dip the cushion cover in cold-water dye.

three

FELT

Felt making

Soft and warm, hand-made felt is also malleable and sculptural, combining all the advantages of beauty, versatility and practicality. Both ancient and modern, felt crosses all boundaries and is as useful and appealing in a contemporary apartment as in its traditional home on the Central Asian plains.

Felt is the oldest form of textile on earth and one of the simplest to create – a combination of fleece, hot water and agitation will produce a unique fabric made of bonded fibres that will not unravel, even if cut. The first felt-makers (probably around 8,500 years ago) were the nomadic people of Central Asia, who used felt as housing and clothing. Collapsible tents, often called 'yurts', were covered with large pieces of felt, some of which were decorated with colourful appliqué. Inside were flooring, cushions, storage and bedding all made from felt, while their owners wore felt hats, boots, cloaks and gloves. Indeed, so important was felt to the nomads that by the fourth century BC their territory was known to the Chinese as 'the land of felt'.

Even today felt is still essential to the lives of the remaining nomadic communities of Turkmenistan, Uzbekistan, Kyrgyzstan and parts of Mongolia and China, who make their yurts, carpets, bags, saddles and cloaks from felt, in patterns and colours that have been handed down from generation to generation. At the end of each summer, the women wash the fleece and beat it with willow sticks, dye it and layer the fibres onto a reed mat. After a sprinkling of hot water and soap, the mat is rolled up, ready to be kicked and rolled around, or dragged behind horses across the steppes.

From Central Asia, the practice of felt-making spread west towards Europe, Scandinavia and eventually South America. Felt's protective properties made it a useful fabric for lining metal armour, and in the late Middle Ages the Cossack armies were known as the 'felt troops' because of the amount of felt that they wore. It was actually only in the 1950s that the Turkish military stopped wearing felt boots. Roman soldiers also wore felt, in the form of tunics, armour and boots, and at the preserved Italian city of Pompeii a wall painting is probably the oldest surviving illustration of felt-making. The Icelandic sagas describe how felt was used to make saddles, while during the French revolution the Jacobeans wore a felt cap as a symbol of freedom and in the early 20th century Cornish tin miners protected their heads with stiffened felt helmets.

As industrialization became more prevalent, the practice of hand-making felt declined in most societies. In recent years, however, craftspeople around the world have developed it as a modern medium that combines both artistry and practicality, developing its potentials by blending wool with other natural fibres, such as camel, alpaca, silk, cashmere and linen, and exploring the uses of natural and synthetic dyes for soft or vibrant effects. Today, hand-made felt makes a welcome appearance in 21st-century life in the form of rugs, throws, cushions, wall hangings and blankets, valued for its fluid, organic appearance, its wonderfully soft, warm texture and its dual qualities of function and beauty.

Table runners are increasingly fashionable, and there is no better way to add tactile appeal to a dining table than with a gorgeous runner made from the softest wool in subtle, sophisticated colours.

Table runner

you will need

(To make a runner measuring about 30 x 200cm)
- Four pieces of synthetic netting, each 1m x 1.8m
- Measuring tape or ruler
- Tailor's chalk or pencil
- 1kg natural wool fibre (tops), such as Blue-Faced Leicester, Jacob or Merino
- 100g of one or a mix of other natural fibres (tops) such as cashmere, silk, camel or alpaca
- Fine darning needle
- Strong, thin wool thread
- Fabric detergent
- Rubber gloves
- Sewing machine (or large needle)
- Thread to match your fibres

The process of making felt by hand may be thousands of years old, but the results can appear surprisingly modern – perhaps thanks to the fashion for all things natural and organic around the home. Our table runner has a wonderfully natural look, with its uneven edges, silky surface and deliberately visible seams. If you prefer a neater style, however, just trim the edges and sew the seams invisibly. As another alternative, do not sew the rectangles together, but use them as individual placemats, or make smaller versions to use as coasters.

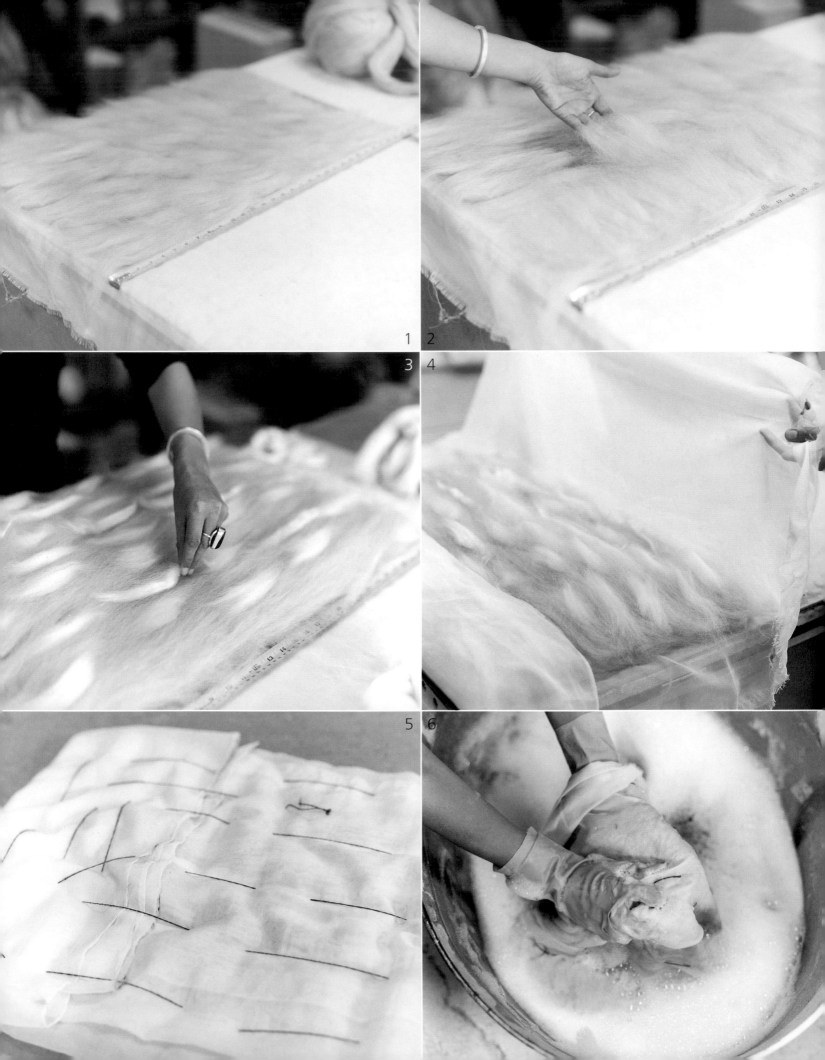

how to make:
Table runner

1 Lay out one piece of netting on a flat surface and, using the tape or ruler and chalk, mark out a rectangle 45 x 75cm. (This will make a finished piece of felt measuring 30 x 50cm – to make a different size, add 50 per cent to the measurements you require, to allow for shrinkage.) Start laying out the wool fibres within the rectangle. Pull fine handfuls of fibres from the end of the roll and lay them all running from left to right, close to each other and overlapping slightly, until the whole rectangle is covered with a fine layer of fibres.

2 Add another layer of wool fibres on top, this time laying them all running in the opposite direction, from top to bottom within the rectangle. This will begin to create a woven build-up of fibres.

3 Keep building up the layers, until you have about five layers, or a dense build-up of fibres. Then, on the top layer, work in the contrasting fibres. Add them across the top layer in long strips. You can create a very even or a more spontaneous and irregular design.

4 Fold the netting over the top to cover, containing the fibres inside.

5 Tack the netting into place with the strong woollen thread. Fold this into three so that it is more manageable to work with. Repeat from step 1 to make another three pieces to the same dimensions.

6 Run a few centimetres of very hot (but not boiling) water into a sink or large container and add a cup of washing liquid or powder. If using powder, it must be well dissolved. Place the four bundles into the water and, wearing rubber gloves, beat and squeeze the bundles vigorously with your hands. At regular intervals, as the fibres absorb the water and the water cools, add a burst of very hot tap water to assist the felting process. After about 20 minutes, you will feel that the bundles have each started to form a dense, well-integrated piece of fabric. Remove the netting – remembering that the felt may still be a little delicate – and continue to wash the pieces (they will still shrink and felt further). At this stage, you can pull the pieces into shape and control how well-felted their surfaces become. This process usually takes around 30–40 minutes (for all four pieces).

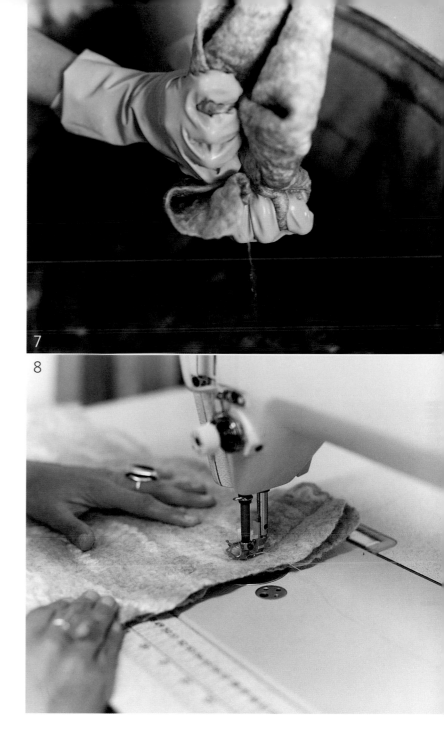

7 Rinse thoroughly in cool water and squeeze out as much excess water as you can. Place each piece on a flat surface and gently pull into an even rectangular shape. If a piece needs more work, wash it again for a little longer. Allow to dry (flat if possible) away from direct heat.

8 Use a sewing machine or a large needle to stitch together the four pieces of felt. Sew along the short edges of the pieces, with the wrong sides facing. If you wish to make more of a feature of the seams – for a more rustic and textured look – you can overstitch by hand using coloured thread and blanket stitch (see page 87).

This impressive rug would be ideal beside a bed or in front of a fire. Created from the softest, warmest materials, it feels immensely cosy and gives a welcoming touch of colour and texture.

Striped rug

Although this rug is a fairly ambitious project, it is not as difficult as it looks. Get a feel for it by experimenting with simpler items such as the table runner on page 136, and you should have no problem at all. In fact, you will probably want to go on to increasingly complex versions. For a larger rug, make three more of the same size and stitch together; you may also want to try different fibres in order to produce a variety of surface patterns. The possibilities are endless, and enormously rewarding.

you will need

(To make a rug measuring about 70 x 100cm)

- A piece of synthetic netting 2m x 2.5m
- Measuring tape or ruler
- Tailor's chalk or pencil
- 1.5kg natural-coloured merino wool fibre (tops)
- 500g merino wool fibre (tops) in three different colours (this project used dusty pink, red and burgundy)
- Fine darning needle
- Strong, thin wool thread
- Fabric detergent
- Rubber gloves

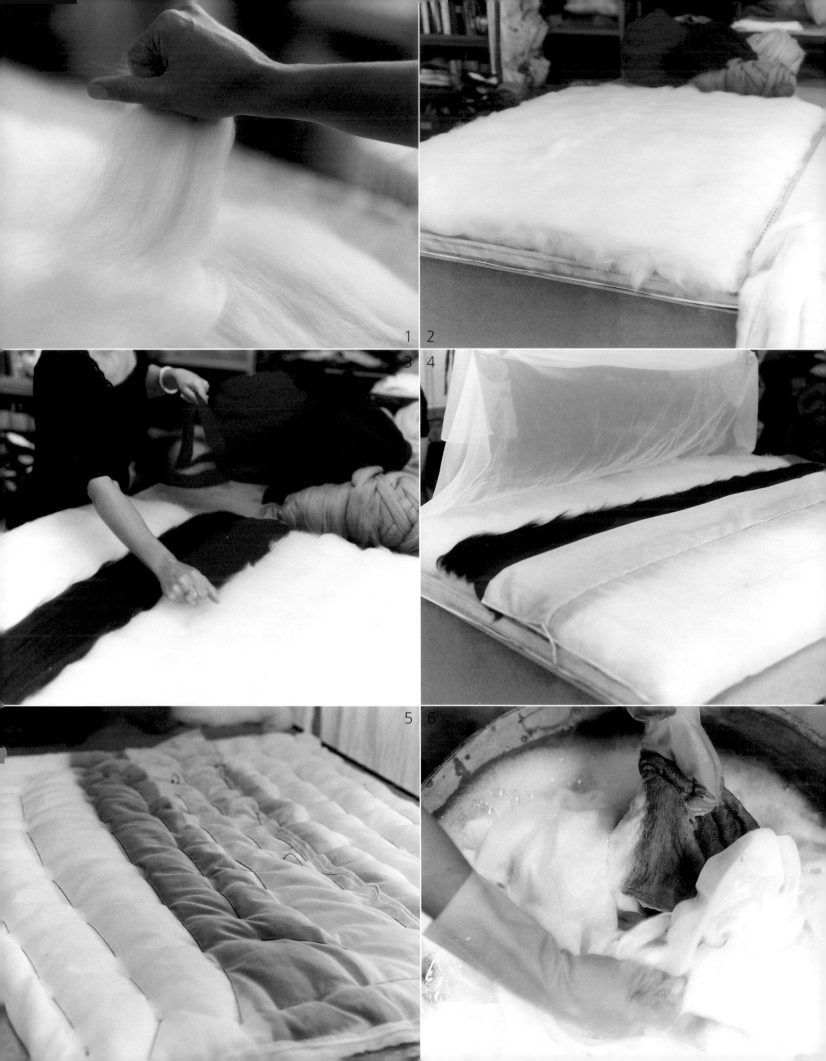

how to make:
Striped rug

1 Lay out the netting on a flat surface and mark out a rectangle 105 x 150cm. (This will make a finished piece of felt measuring 70 x 100cm – to make a different size, add 50 per cent to the measurements you require, to allow for shrinkage.) Start laying out the merino fibres within the rectangle – pull fine handfuls of fibres from the end of the roll and lay them all running from left to right, close to each other and overlapping slightly, until the whole rectangle is covered with a fine layer of fibres.

2 Add another layer of merino fibres on top, this time laying them all running from top to bottom within the rectangle. Begin to create a woven build-up of fibres.

3 Build up the layers until you have at least eight layers or a very dense build-up of fibres. Then add the coloured fibres, placing them across the top layer in long stripes, alternating the colours to create blocks in varying widths.

4 Fold the netting carefully over the top to cover, containing the fibres inside.

5 Tack the netting into place using the strong woollen thread. Roll or fold the felt 'parcel' lengthways so it is more manageable to work with.

6 Run a few centimetres of very hot (but not boiling) water into a sink or large container and add a cup of detergent. If using powder, it must be well dissolved. Place the roll into the water and, wearing rubber gloves, beat and squeeze it with your hands. At regular intervals, as the fibres absorb the water and the water cools, add a burst of very hot tap water to assist the process. After about 30 minutes, you will feel that the roll has started to form a dense, well-integrated piece of fabric. Remove the netting and unroll the piece – the felt may still be delicate – then continue to wash it. At this stage, you can pull it into shape and control how well-felted the surface becomes. This entire process usually takes around 40–60 minutes (leave it in the water for a while if it becomes too tiring, and return to it later).

7 Rinse thoroughly in cool water and squeeze out as much excess water as you can.

8 Place on a flat surface and pull into an even, rectangular shape. Allow to dry (flat if possible) naturally.

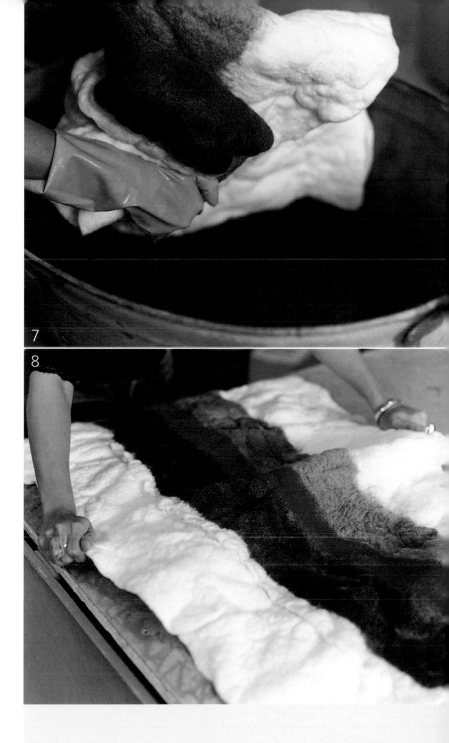

working with fibres
To avoid holes or thin patches in your finished felt, layer the fibres as evenly and thoroughly as possible. The finer the fibres you use, the easier the felting process will be – and the more delicate the finished piece.

Using felt

In the 19th century it became possible to produce lengths of uniform felt by machine. The fabric has been used in thousands of ways ever since and, although many of its uses have been mundane, for some craftspeople it has become the vehicle for expression, innovation and experimentation.

The practicality and versatility of felt have been known to man since the seventh millennium BC, and making felt by hand, using woollen fibres, water, heat and agitation has been practised ever since. Felt making was a cottage industry, however, until the arrival of industrialization in the 19th century. As wool manufacture became mechanized, so too did that of felt, initially as a means of using up waste wool, but later as a trade in its own right. By the middle of the 19th century, factories in the industrialized world were capable of producing large quantities of felt in long lengths of uniform quality, in different thicknesses and dyed (synthetically) in a rainbow of hues.

For the newly developed machine industry, felt was invaluable, and was used for shock and sound absorption, lining, sealing, air filtration, weather and dust shielding, heat and cold insulation, padding and packing. It was also used by hat makers, and went in and out of fashion as a garment fabric. It has periodically been made into coats, capes, jackets and skirts (its most recent incarnation being the duffel coat) as well as, in Finland, boots and socks.

The advantages of industrially produced felt did not stop there, however, and it soon came to be used all around the home, too. Its many applications – a great number of them still as relevant now as they were then – include roofing, carpet underlay and printed top carpets (a speciality of the late-19th century), piano dampeners, billiard tables, upholstery, table covers, cabinet linings, curtains and, of course, blankets and throws. Even from the mid-20th century, when synthetics such as nylon and rayon began to emerge as serious competitors for natural fabrics, felt never completely disappeared – it was simply too useful a fabric.

In the 1960s and '70s, craftspeople in Europe and America discovered the appeal of sheet felt for domestic hobbies. Here was a unique material that was tough and soft, strong and yet malleable. It was available in long lengths and small squares, in a range of thicknesses and an almost infinite number of vivid colours, and it could be cut without fraying, embossed, punched, stitched, glued, stuffed, sculpted and painted. Enthusiasm grew for making children's toys and games, in particular, from felt, and it was a favourite material for patterns in craft instruction books. The fashion waned in the 1980s and early '90s, but at the end of the 20th century, felt enjoyed a renaissance, re-entering the fashion arena as a fabric that offered huge potential for experimentation. In recent years, craftspeople have begun to see machine-made felt in a new light, as both environmentally friendly and avant-garde, and are using it in astonishing new ways – cutting, tearing, stretching, stitching and manipulating it into unexpected incarnations and giving a familiar fabric an exciting, modern twist.

Sometimes the simplest of projects can be the most effective, and what is so nice about this one is, indeed, its utter simplicity, resulting in work that has great subtlety but also quiet impact.

Wall hanging

you will need

(To make a hanging measuring about 40 x 180cm)

- 15 x 45cm piece of 6mm-thick hard taupe felt
- Cutting mat
- Metal ruler
- Rotating cutter
- 44 x 187cm semi-transparent ivory fabric (not too flimsy – nylon sailcloth is ideal)
- Iron
- Pins
- Sewing machine with a strong needle
- Thread to match the fabric
- Scissors
- Masking tape
- Pen
- Length of bamboo or wooden dowelling (to fit the hanging) and hooks

The qualities of manufactured felt are completely different to those of its hand-made counterpart. Available in a wide range of colours and thicknesses, it offers plenty of possibilities for craftspeople – the trick is to make the most of its regularity without being hindered by it. Very straightforward to complete, this wall hanging has a subtle, tactile appeal, in neutral colours that would work with any style of décor. In addition, it could easily be made larger or hung with several others to act as a striking door screen or a room divider.

how to make: **Wall hanging**

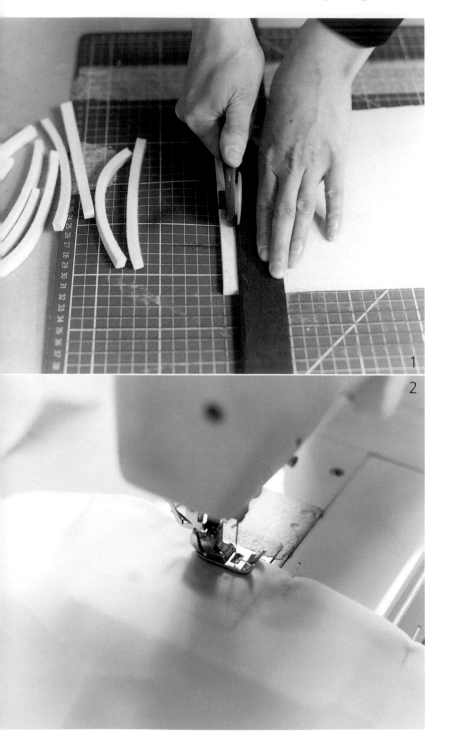

1 Place the felt on a cutting mat and use a metal ruler and a rotating cutter to cut 40 strips of felt measuring 1cm by 15cm. Work with care when using the cutter.

2 Take the transparent fabric and turn the edges in by 1cm, then another 1cm. Press, pin, then stitch. Turn the top edge over by about 5cm and stitch again, close to the edge.

3 Stick the masking tape in two straight lines down the length of the fabric, about 10cm from the left and 15cm from the right, leaving a gap measuring 15cm in the middle.

4 Make sure that you smooth down the masking tape firmly as you flatten it down the length of the fabric. Make certain also that there are no creases in the fabric below.

5 On the tape, mark the positions for your strips of felt, starting about 20cm from the top edge and leaving a gap of about 1.5cm between each one. Mark a group of 10, then leave a gap of 15cm, then mark another group of 10, and so on.

6 Align your first strip with the top marking, and attach it to the fabric by stitching along its central line (5cm each side hangs free from the fabric). Repeat until the fabric is covered with strips. Pull off the masking tape. Press, if necessary, then simply push the bamboo through the large hem at the top and hang.

1

2

variations
If you wish to vary the design of your wall hanging, you could dye the strips of felt in different colours using cold-water dyes, or cut them to different lengths, or stitch a large rectangle of contrasting fabric beneath the felt strips.

3 4

5 6

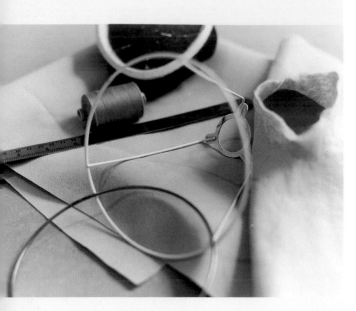

This unusual lampshade is made using a combination of techniques, and while each is individually simple, the end result is complex and intriguing. This is a project with real character and impact.

Funnel lampshade

you will need

(To make a lampshade 40cm high and about 15.5cm diameter)
- Two rectangles of very pale mint green flame-retardant display felt, 40 x 50cm
- Steam iron
- Scissors
- Sewing machine
- Thread to match the felt
- Pins
- Metal craft ring (15.5cm diameter)
- Needle and thread (or a hot glue gun)
- Lampshade holder (15.5cm diameter)

Not only can felt be cut without fraying, but it can also be stretched, stitched and layered with ease, allowing for some really unusual effects. What is more, thin sheets of machine-made felt are very slightly transparent, and so lend themselves well to playing with light and shade. When making this lampshade, remember that the same pattern could also be put to use as a floor lamp or a pendant light; you could also choose thread in a contrasting colour for the delicate stitching that emphasizes its unusual shape.

how to make: Funnel lampshade

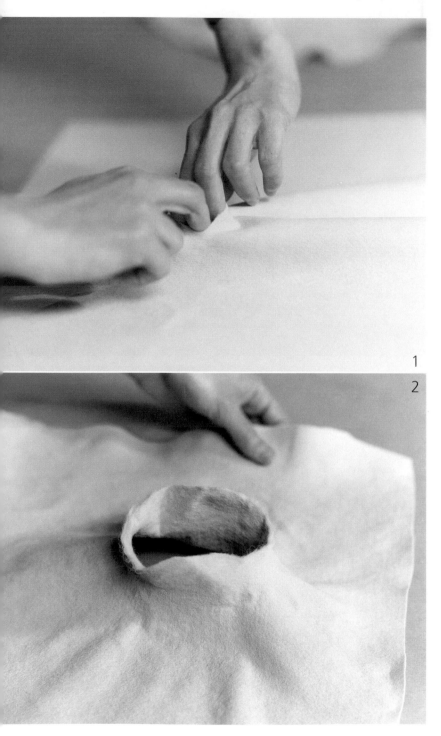

1

2

1 Press both pieces of felt with a steam iron. Take one piece and snip a hole in the centre, about 2cm wide. Start to pull it out with your fingers, stretching the felt evenly to enlarge the hole a little. Be gentle or the felt may rip. Hold an edge of the fabric and pull on the central cylinder shape to make it protrude further. Every now and then, put the felt on a flat surface and flatten the edges.

2 Pull until the central cylinder is about 7cm in diameter and about 5cm high. Trim the top edge of the cylinder to even it out, and flatten the surrounding area.

3 Turn the top edge of the cylinder in about 5mm and machine stitch a hem about 3mm from the edge. Turn inside out and trim the hem close to the stitching. Turn out.

4 Align the sewing machine foot with the hem you have just sewn, and begin to stitch in a spiral shape around the cylinder. Do not worry about making this too neat. Keep going round and round until you have covered the 5cm height of the cylinder or, if you wish to make it more elaborate, carry on stitching around the flat portion of felt. Lay the stitched felt on the other, plain piece, and pin together around the edges. Stitch two lines through both layers either side of the cylinder, and another two either side of the centre of the cylinder. Stitch in a circle around the base of the cylinder. Press, avoiding the cylinder.

5 Stitch both layers together along the two long sides, very close to the edges. Fold the two short sides together, right sides together, to make a drum shape, and stitch along this seam through all four layers, close to the edge. Press, without flattening the cylinder, and turn out.

6 Insert the metal ring into the bottom of the shade and turn the edge of the felt over it by about 1cm. Hand stitch invisibly or use a glue gun. Repeat with the lampshade holder, inserting it at the top of the shade. Place the shade on the base, making sure the felt is away from light source.

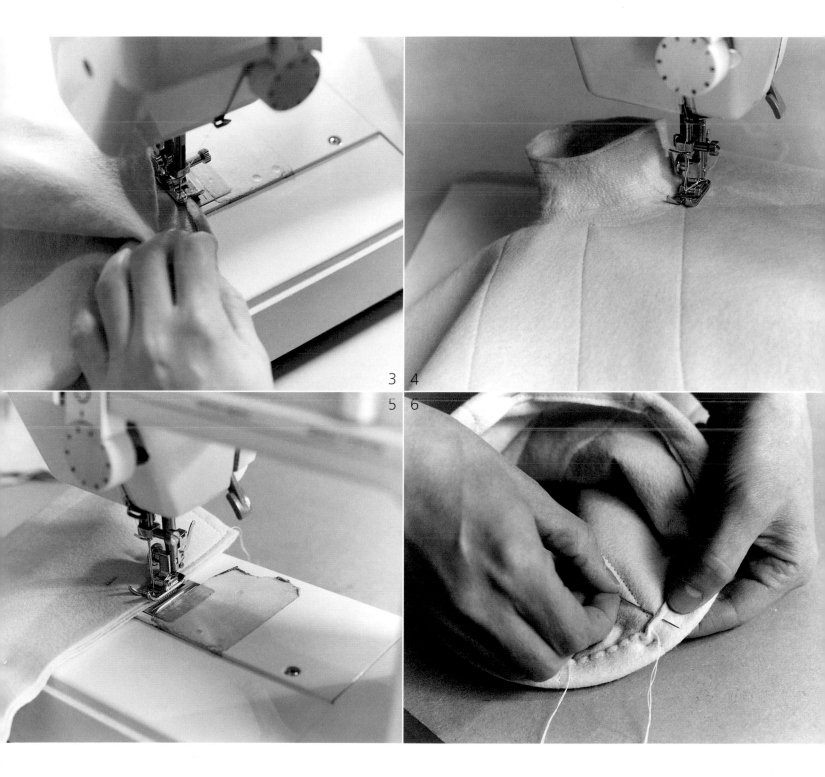

3 4

5 6

four

WEAVING & BEADING

Weaving

From the simplest plain weave to twill, damask, satin, velvet and tapestry, weaving is one of our most ancient crafts – the essential means of producing textiles for warmth and clothing. More than that, however, it can be a delightful way of exploring colour, pattern and texture in two, or even three, dimensions.

When early man began to settle in primitive dwellings and to farm animals, it became possible to set up looms and weave cloth. It is even likely that weaving predates spinning as, though most weaving uses spun thread, it can also be performed with natural materials, such as raffia. Although very simple weaving can be done with the fingers, the earliest type of loom was the warp-weighted loom, where the vertical threads were hung from a horizontal beam and tied to weights of clay or stone. Illustrated on Greek vases from the sixth to fourth centuries BC, these looms were found all over Northern Europe before the Roman conquest, and were still used in Scandinavia until the 20th century.

As different looms were developed around the world, so the art of weaving varied from place to place and time to time. In 4,500BC Egypt, very fine linen was woven on a horizontal loom for use as burial shrouds. Later, the Egyptians became adept at colourful tapestry weaving, for everyday clothing and for decoration. In India and South-East Asia the backstrap, or body-tension loom, became important, as it was able to produce a wide variety of complex patterns. It was the treadle loom, however, used for silk weaving in China as long ago as the third century BC, that took the art of weaving one step further. This made the technique faster and allowed longer pieces of cloth –

indeed, many hand weavers still use this type of loom today. The draw loom, which may also have originated in China but was developed in the Middle East in the sixth and seventh centuries, allowed even more complex and varied patterning. It was widely used until the early-19th century, when it was replaced by the mechanical Jacquard loom.

Over the centuries, various countries have been pre-eminent in the art of weaving. Beautiful fabrics were produced in Persia from the third century onwards, and then in Spain and Southern Italy under Islamic rule. Later, Italian silks were most highly desired – those from Lucca were lavishly embellished with metallic thread, while Venetian and Florentine velvets were widely exported. When the silk industry established itself at Lyons, France, in the 16th century, it became the chief centre for European silk weaving. England too, established a reputation for woven wool and silk, thanks especially to an influx of skilled Flemish and Huguenot refugees in the 16th and 17th centuries.

With the advent of mechanization in the 18th century, hand weaving virtually disappeared in many Western areas, until it was stimulated by a revival of interest in the late-1800s. Gradually, weaving workshops and guilds were set up, and the craft enjoyed a renaissance. No longer employed for widespread production of clothing and domestic textiles, now hand weaving is an artistic medium in which hand-made character can be enjoyed, traditional processes rediscovered and new methods explored.

Weaving need not involve only traditional threads – you can weave practically anything long and slender. This project employs silver-plated wire to unusual and extraordinary effect.

Fringed lampshade

you will need

(To make 50cm of braid, 15cm deep, including tassels of about 10cm)

- 5cm-wide ribbon, long enough to wind around the base of your shade
- Plain white lampshade (fabric, paper or plastic)
- Frame – a square/rectangular tapestry frame from a craft supplier, a stretcher from a picture frame or even a chair back or ladder. It should measure at least 20cm wide; the other length will determine how long you can weave each length of braid
- Reel of strong cotton (the type used for beading is ideal)
- Scissors
- Masking tape
- 2 x 500gsm of 0.5mm diameter 25swg silver-plated copper wire (wire A)
- Old scissors or pliers
- Ruler
- 40 skeins silver embroidery silk
- A4 card
- 1 x 500gsm of 0.25mm diameter 33swg silver-plated copper wire (wire B)
- Needle and thread (or PVA, if the shade is made of paper or plastic)

For a quirky contrast to a plain lampshade, this woven trim has the perfect note of glamorous eccentricity. It uses a mixture of wire and thread, achieving an effect that is ethereal and decorative but with an avant-garde edge. The weaving technique, however, is very straightforward – it is called 'plain weave'. This involves only working the weft inserts over and under the warp, backwards and forwards until you have created a trim to the depth you require.

This woven trimming adds texture, colour and style to an otherwise plain and simple roller blind. Though designed according to the traditional principles of the craft, it is fun and frivolous, too.

Trimmed blind

you will need

(To make 50cm of braid, 12cm deep, including 7cm tassels)

- Measuring tape
- Plain fabric roller or roman blind
- Frame (see page 158)
- Reel of strong cotton (will not break with a light tug – the type used for beading is ideal)
- Scissors
- Masking tape
- 24 skeins embroidery silk in ivory
- 24 skeins embroidery silk in silver
- 6 skeins embroidery silk in burnt orange
- A4 card
- Pins
- Needle and thread (or PVA)

Although it appears distinctly untraditional, this project involves techniques that would be recognized by weavers from centuries ago. How far you want to go is up to you. You could, as here, leave the weft ends long and uneven for an organic look, or cut them short and neat for a style that's more ordered. Crucial to the success of the project, however, is the choice of colours – cool silver with burnt orange has the right mix of sophistication and surprise, though you could, of course, substitute any colours of your choice.

Ribbonwork

Ribbons have always had symbolic meaning, representing love and friendship, remembrance or achievement, rank and status or military prowess. Just as importantly, though, they make unique decorations, pretty and precious, subtle or sumptuous, with which to adorn clothing and home furnishings of all types.

The art of *passementerie*, or decorative textile trimming, dates back to the ancient civilizations of Greece, Rome, Egypt, China and South America – where decorative trimmings were placed in temples and the tombs of royalty and chiefs. In Medieval France it was highly esteemed and, as long ago as the 13th century, guilds had been established for the craftsmen who made embellishments for pillow slips, women's head dresses, tapestries, flags and church textiles. By the 17th century, as domestic textiles became more prevalent (in the form of curtains and upholstered furniture), passementerie was used increasingly around the home.

Decoration for its own sake was the fashion during the 18th century, and lavish adornments of all kinds were in vogue among royalty and the upper classes. Silk ribbons had by now become a favourite, in the form of bows and ruching on bodices, robes, sleeves, hats, shoes and embroidery, and in both France and England they came to represent nobility. In fact, in England laws were passed that forbade the wearing of ribbons by anyone except the aristocracy. At first, ribbons were woven individually on hand looms, but mechanized weaving brought about a breakthrough: advanced looms could weave any number of ribbons at once, and in all manner of beautifully intricate patterns.

The first American ribbon factory was established in 1815, but it was some time before ribbons became widely popular with the settlers, as they were associated with their English rulers. Native Americans, on the other hand, had been introduced to ribbons by traders, and used them on shirts and skirts in colourful, abstract patterns.

The 19th century saw a resurgence of interest in ribbons in both America and Europe, and from the late 1800s numerous magazines offered instruction in ribbon embroidery and embellishments – for many purposes, including hair ornaments, belts, bags, parasols, hats, gloves, lingerie, ballgowns, pillows, firescreens and quilts. But as lifestyles changed, and both clothing and home décor became simpler, such extravagances were seen as outdated. By the First World War, the use of ribbons had declined, until eventually they were associated mainly with babies' clothing, lingerie and special-occasion dresses.

In recent years, however, the variety of ribbons available has increased dramatically, and there has been a corresponding revival in ribbon trims and decoration. Craftspeople use them in projects ranging from cushions and throws to gift wrapping and Christmas decorations, often hand in hand with embroidery, appliqué and beading, but sometimes simply as an end in themselves. The techniques employed range from weaving and appliqué to making rosettes and tassels, adding a unique and attractive decorative aesthetic and transforming the plain and ordinary into something utterly extraordinary.

Unusual ribbons are available in all kinds of textures and colours, and this project makes good use of them to create a woven cushion cover with a simple tie closure that is both functional and decorative.

Chequered cushion

This attractive project is really feminine, yet its neat criss-cross pattern gives it a bold look that is slightly plainer than some ribbonwork, while the crisp piped edging adds a clean, professional finish. Instead of fiddly zips or buttons, it features a simple overlap with a tie fastening made from matching ribbons. Sophisticated, muted colours have a contemporary appeal, though of course you could choose any hue to contrast with or complement your interior.

you will need

(To make a 35cm square cushion)
- Scissors
- 1m silk (at least 49cm wide) in ivory/taupe
- Measuring tape or ruler
- 5.5m each of two organza ribbons in coordinating or contrasting colours (this project used ivory and mid-brown), 2.8cm wide
- Pins
- Needle
- Tacking thread
- Sewing machine (a zipper foot is helpful but not essential)
- Sewing thread to match the silk
- Iron
- 1.45m fancy-edge tape, 0.4cm wide, to match the silk
- 1.45m piping cord
- Tailor's chalk
- 35cm square cushion pad

1 2

3 4

5 6

how to make:
Chequered cushion

1 Cut the silk into a 39cm square, and three rectangles measuring 27 x 39cm, 26 x 39cm and 10cm x 1m. Cut the organza ribbons to 13 lengths of 39cm in each colour and two lengths of 20cm in each colour. Lay the 39cm square piece of silk on a flat surface. Place 13 ribbons on top, running from left to right and butting up to each other, alternating the colours. Pin, then tack them to the left edge of the silk.

2 Place 13 more ribbons on top of the fabric, over the previous set and this time running from top to bottom, again alternating the colours. Pin and then tack them to the top edge of the silk. Start to weave the ribbons one by one, under and over alternating ribbons, pulling them squarely into place as you go. When all the ribbons are woven, pin then tack them to the bottom and right edges of the silk.

3 For the piping, take the silk rectangle measuring 10cm x 1m and cut it in half lengthways. Place the right sides together and stitch down one short side with the sewing machine, leaving 1cm seam allowance. Press open (on a low temperature). You should have a rectangle measuring 5 x 198cm — now cut it down so it measures 5 x 145cm. Pin and then stitch the fancy-edge tape to the right side of this piece, in the centre. Fold the piece in half lengthways, wrong sides together, and press. Then fold the piece around the piping cord and pin together, enclosing the piping. Stitch all the way along, as close to the piping cord inside as possible (a zipper foot is useful here, but not essential).

4 With the tailor's chalk, mark a 35cm square in the centre of your woven-ribbon panel, on the right side. Lay the piping around this, with its raw edges to the outside, and pin (clipping the seam allowance at the corners), then tack. Stitch it on (again, a zipper foot is useful), as close to the piping cord as possible.

5 To make the back of the cushion, take the two remaining silk rectangles. On both, take one of the edges that measures 39cm and turn it over by 1cm, and then again by 4cm. Press, pin and stitch.

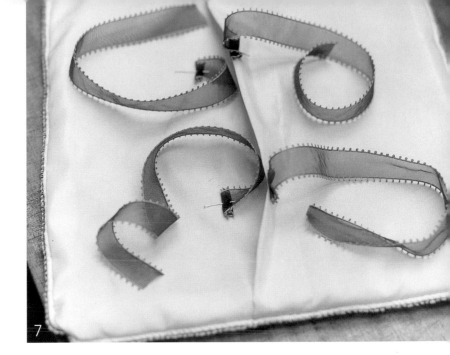

6 Place the woven-ribbon panel right-side up on a flat surface. Place the two other silk rectangles right side down on top of it, with their hemmed edges in the centre, overlapping by 4cm. Pin and then tack together around the edges. Stitch together, 1mm outside the piping. Turn out.

7 Press the cushion cover carefully, with the iron on a low temperature. Stitch the two pairs of 20cm-long ribbons to either side of the opening, equidistant from the centre, insert the cushion pad and tie the ribbons together with simple knots or bows. (Smart, symmetrical bows will make the underside of the cushion look almost as beautiful as the woven top.)

neat weaving
Make sure that you keep your weaving as tidy and flat as possible to prevent it bagging later. As you move across the cushion, check that the tension remains consistent and, if necessary, go back and tidy up at the end. The flatter the finish, the more professional the look.

Careful application of the piping also adds to the quality of the final cushion. Make sure your sewing is neat so that the piping creates an attractive border around the cushion.

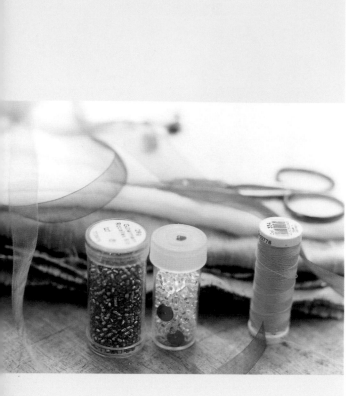

This gorgeous woven-ribbon bag, embellished with sparkly beads and sequins, is just the right size for a glamorous girls' night out.

Ribbon bag

you will need

(To make a bag measuring 20 x 30cm)
- Scissors
- 5.2m organza ribbon in pale green, 1.5cm wide (A)
- 4.3m organza ribbon in mid-blue, 1.5cm wide (B)
- 9m organza ribbon in mid-green, 2.5cm wide (C)
- Measuring tape
- Four pieces of silk dupion, in citron green, two measuring 37 x 50cm and two measuring 8 x 43cm
- Pins
- Needle
- Tacking thread
- 20–25 coordinating beads
- 20–25 coordinating sequins
- Iron
- Four pieces of iron-on interfacing measuring 37 x 50cm, 6 x 37cm and two of 3 x 40cm
- Sewing machine
- Thread to match the silk
- 1m taffeta ribbon in dark green, 2.5cm wide
- Button
- Thread to match the button

The organza ribbons that are interwoven to create this project give it an air of delicacy and softness, but with its silk backing and iron-on interfacing the bag is robust enough to withstand a night on the town. When you are making it, simply ensure that the ribbons are straight and butting up to each other neatly, and the rest of the project will be simplicity itself. If you wish, instead of the button-and-loop fastening, you could add a tie fastening with two ribbons, or an internal magnetic popper.

1 2

3 4

5 6

how to make:
Ribbon bag

1 Cut the three organza ribbons into lengths – A into five lengths of 50cm and seven lengths of 37cm; B into four lengths of 50cm and six lengths of 37cm and C into nine lengths of 50cm and twelve lengths of 37cm. Lay one silk dupion rectangle measuring 37 x 50cm on a flat surface. Place the 50cm-long ribbons on top of it, butting up to each other, alternating the colours as follows: ACBCACBC. Pin and then tack them to one edge of the silk.

2 Place the 37cm-long ribbons on top of the fabric, over the previous set and running in the opposite direction. Alternate the colours as before. Pin and then tack them to one edge of the silk. Start to weave the ribbons one by one, under and over alternating ribbons, pulling them squarely into place as you go. When all the ribbons are woven, pin then tack them to the remaining two edges of the silk.

3 Neatly sew some beads and sequins to the surface of the woven ribbons, in a chequerboard pattern.

4 Iron the 6 x 37cm interfacing across the middle of the back of the woven-ribbon panel. Fold in half lengthways with the right sides together; pin then stitch the two sides, leaving a 2cm seam allowance. Stitch diagonally across the two bottom corners, 3cm away from the corner points.

5 Cut, about 1.5cm away from the stitching. Press the seams open and neatly turn out.

6 For the lining, iron the 37 x 50cm interfacing to the other 37 x 50cm silk dupion rectangle. Fold in half (bringing the two short sides together), with the right sides together – pin then stitch the two sides, leaving a 2cm seam allowance. Stitch diagonally across the two bottom corners and cut (as before). Press the seams open. Put the lining inside the outer bag.

7 To make the handles, first cut the taffeta ribbon into two 50cm lengths. Take one of the silk dupion rectangles measuring 8 x 43cm. Fold in half along the length and press, then fold in 1cm on each edge and press again. Iron the interfacing to the inside of one half, and stitch the taffeta ribbon to the top of the other side. Stitch neatly along the two edges, on the right side.

7

8

8 Take a short length of the remaining 1.5cm organza ribbon, fold it in half and stitch it together, making a loop large enough for your button. This will be the fastening for your bag, so check that it is positioned correctly. Insert the loop and tack it between the lining and the outer bag. Then tack the two handles between the lining and the outer bag. Turn in the top edges of the lining and outer bag by about 2cm each. Press, pin and tack. Stitch neatly around the rim of the bag, just below the top on the right side. To finish, sew on the button securely, opposite the loop.

Beadwork

Beads have been made throughout human history, all over the world, from a huge variety of materials – from bones to wood, glass to stones, shells to seeds. They have been used as trade goods, prayer aids, magical protectors, indicators of status and, of course, as eye-catching adornment for clothing and other objects.

Beads have been around for as long as man: the earliest known examples, made from teeth and bone to be worn as pendants, date back to around 38,000BC. Basic beads would have been fashioned from whatever materials were to hand, but even as long ago as the third or fourth century BC, a method of mass-producing glass beads was developed in South-East India, and later spread to Vietnam, Thailand, Malaysia, Indonesia and Sri Lanka. The resulting tiny, doughnut-shaped beads were probably strung as necklaces, woven or sewn onto cloth, and were traded all over the globe for 2,000 years.

Ancient Egypt was another centre for beads, which were hand-made from stone and, later, glass, to adorn garments for everyday wear and funerary purposes. But beads were not only used for decoration. The name 'bead' comes from the old English 'bede', which means 'prayer', and the meditative nature of counting beads has for centuries given them a religious purpose. They have also had superstitious and symbolic meaning – to ward off evil or attract fertility, or imply purity, power, friendship or love. And, of course, they have been used for trade, by nomadic tribes who found them a convenient method of carrying wealth, and by Europeans who used them to deal with the peoples of Africa, Asia and America. Dutch traders, for example, bought the island of Manhattan with beads worth the equivalent of 24 dollars.

In the late 16th century, small glass beads were introduced to the Native Americans, who used them for necklaces and woven or sewn borders on clothing and other objects, in colourful, geometric patterns. This type of work is one of the predominant beadcraft forms today. African beadwork, too, is an important example of the craft. Stone, clay, shells, gems, coral, glass and metal were all used by African tribes to fashion beads. But it was the import of millions of glass beads from Venice and Bohemia in the late-15th century that transformed African beadwork, giving rise to traditions such as the beaded sculpture of the Grassfields region of Cameroon, the elaborate clothing and necklaces of the Maasai, and the abstract compositions of Ndebele garments.

In Europe, the use of beads reached its height during the Renaissance. The less well-off were forbidden to decorate themselves with beads and ribbons, but for wealthy people beaded clothing was a sign of status and good taste. Beadwork also boomed in Victorian times, when leisured ladies spent their time stitching samplers and other items. Since then people all around the world have continued to be fascinated by beads, using glass, stone, wood, china, pearls and other materials, small and large, plain or multi-coloured, as an artistic, decorative and alluring way of embellishing clothing, home furnishings and all kinds of precious objects.

This project needs nothing other than a length of organza as wide as your window, a scattering of imitation pearls in various sizes and a little sewing skill for fabulous results.

Sheer curtain

you will need

- Scissors
- Length of organza cut to fit your window, allowing 2cm each side for seams, 10cm at the top for hanging and 20cm at the bottom for a hem
- Measuring tape
- Iron
- Pins
- Tacking thread
- Needle
- Sewing machine
- Thread to match the organza
- Embroidery hoop
- Beading needle
- Nylon monofilament thread (clear)
- Imitation pearls in various sizes (this project required five strings each of 4mm and 6mm diameter, ten strings of 7mm and three strings each of 9mm and 12mm)
- Polished rock crystal chips (this project required five strings)
- Dowelling
- Hooks

Sheer curtains are often a necessity, to disguise an unpleasant view or prevent prying eyes from seeing in. But sometimes they can be a delight as well; this example diffuses light softly with the added benefit of a glamorous beaded edging that shimmers gently and also gives the fabric extra weight. The stitching is straightforward – it is the skill in placing the random-sized pearls that gives this project its beautiful, organic appearance. Never have net curtains been this good!

how to make: Cuff bracelet

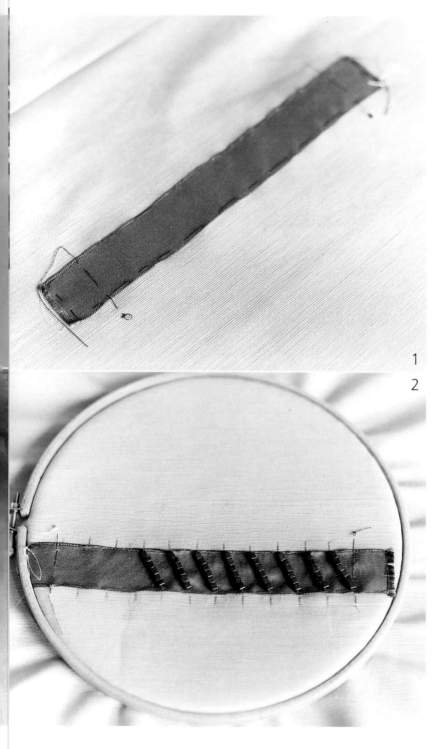

1

2

1 Tack the silk ribbon to the centre of the calico. Measure 2cm in from each end of the ribbon and sew a line of tacking across the ribbon at each of these points. You will only bead between them. Within these lines, use a pencil to mark every 1.5cm on one edge of the ribbon and every 1.25cm on the other edge.

2 Place the calico into the embroidery hoop. With the beading needle threaded double with the monofilament, cast on neatly to the back of the ribbon at the first 1.25cm mark, and bring the needle up to the right side. Thread on approximately six of the larger beads. Take the stitch over to the first 1.5cm mark on the opposite edge, making a slight diagonal, then sew underneath the calico, bringing the needle up on the first edge at the second 1.25cm mark. Thread on six more large beads and continue, sewing diagonally from pencil mark to pencil mark, until the entire ribbon (except for the 2cm at each end) is covered. Leave a little of the ribbon's selvage showing on both sides.

3 Fill in the gaps made by the first beading using the smaller beads (they will partially overlay the first ones and create a rounded effect). Work in a similar way, but this time sew the beads on two diagonals, creating a criss-cross effect. You will need about 13 of the smaller beads to cover a stitch that goes from edge to edge of the ribbon.

4 Allowing an extra 1cm all round, cut the beaded ribbon off the backing fabric. Neatly cut the backing away from the unbeaded ends of the ribbon and turn in the remaining excess fabric. Press and hem neatly by hand.

5 Cover the back of the cuff with the velvet ribbon, and stitch into place. Turn each end over by 1cm then another 1cm, press and stitch neatly all around.

6 With the silk embroidery thread, make two loops in the centre of one end of the cuff, large enough to go over the button. Blanket stitch over both loops to create a fastening. Sew the button onto the other end of the cuff.

3   4
5   6

how to make: **Star decoration**

1

2

1 Soak 12 or 13 willow rods in a bath of cold water for an hour, then wrap them in a damp tea towel and set aside. With the secateurs, cut the dry willow into 35 lengths, each 26cm long. Divide these into five bundles, with seven sticks in each.

2 Take the first and second bundles, place the end of the first bundle on top of the end of the second bundle and hold at a 45 degree angle. Bind them together by taking a wet willow rod and sliding the thin end (tip) through both bundles about 2cm from the top.

3 Wrap the wet rod three times around the two bundles and slide the thick end (butt) up through the bind. It may help to use a bradawl to ease it through. Pull tightly to make it secure.

4 Trim the ends of the willow neatly with the secateurs, so that the points of the star are even. Make sure that you do not trim too close to the binding, however, or you could weaken the joints. Take a third bundle and place over the other end of the second bundle. Hold at a 45-degree angle. Bind the ends together as before and trim them.

5 Take a fourth bundle, and place over the other end of the third bundle – it should be placed across, over the first bundle and under the second bundle. Bind and trim as before. Bind the fifth bundle to the ends of bundles one and four, running over two and under three.

6 Arrange the star so it looks even. Then bind each of the cross sections – take a wet willow rod and slide the tip through the cross section so that it holds. Bring the butt up through the hole in the middle of the star and continue to wrap three times. Slide the butt through the bind and pull tight. Trim off all ends neatly.

3 4
5 6

how to make:
Plant climber

1 On an area of grass or turf, cut the thick (butt) ends of the 12 uprights at a slant with the secateurs. This will make it easier to push them into the ground.

2 Mark a 50cm diameter circle on the ground with an upright (see below), then push the 12 uprights into the ground (butt end first) at even intervals like a clock face. Bring the thin ends (tips) together and tie them with a piece of string.

3 Take a weaver, bend it in half and wrap it around one of the uprights about 30cm from the ground. Take the butt end of the weaver behind the next upright and bring it back to the front.

4 Now take the tip end in front of the second upright, behind the third upright and bring it back to the front. The tension of the weavers will hold them in place.

5 Now join in another weaver. Slide its butt end alongside the butt end of the first weaver and work the two of them together in front of the fourth upright, then behind the fifth upright and back to the front.

6 Keep joining in more weavers at every upright until you are weaving with three or more to make a thick band. Weave three times around the structure, parallel to the ground, before spiralling up to the top, travelling around the uprights three times. Finish about 20cm from the top.

7 Remove the string. Take one thin weaver to bind the top: slide its butt end into the centre of the uprights and, holding them together, bring the tip round 3–4 times, wrapping all the uprights and weavers together. Slide the tip up through the bind and pull it tight.

8 Finish by trimming all the ends of the uprights neatly. If there are any rogue splinters of willow sticking out of any part of the structure, snip them off with the secateurs.

marking a circle
To mark out your 50cm circle, knock a stake into the ground and then tie a 25cm piece of string to it. Tie a length of cane to the other end of the string and move it round the stake, scoring out the circle on the ground.

7

8

They say that texture is the new colour, and these elegant writing papers demonstrate just how attractive a combination of intriguing textures can be.

Writing paper

you will need

(To make 10 sheets of A4 paper)
- Newspapers (at least 10)
- Shallow plastic tray
- Paper-making mould (but not a deckle); the screen area should be about A4 size
- 11 smooth kitchen cloths
- Printers' offcuts or unbleached cartridge paper
- Food blender
- Seeds, dried leaves and grasses
- Washing-up bowl
- One tablespoon wheat starch
- Sponge
- Old book for recycling paper
- Newspapers for recycling paper
- Brown craft paper
- Two wooden boards

To make a stack of lovely writing paper all you need is to add a selection of seeds, leaves and grasses to the basic mix, as is done so well in many Indonesian papers. Ensure that the textural ingredients are not too lumpy, however, or it will be impossible to use the paper for its intended purpose; other than that you can have great fun with choosing which particular extras you like best. Irregular, uneven edges are another lovely touch that give this project a personal and organic look.

how to make:
Writing paper

1 Prepare a couching mound. Fold up five newspapers so that they fit into the tray, stacked with the folded edges on alternate sides. Fill the tray with water until the newspapers are covered and leave until they are completely soaked. Drain off the excess water, then rock the mesh screen of the mould across the top of the newspaper mound so that it has a smooth surface, slightly higher in the middle than at the edges. Cover with a smooth kitchen cloth.

2 If possible, soak the paper in water before you start (this makes it easier but is not essential). Take the printers' offcuts (or your palest coloured paper) and tear into 2.5cm squares. Add a small quantity to a food blender two-thirds full of water, then add a small amount of the seeds, leaves and grasses. Blend for around 10 seconds and pour into a washing-up bowl half full of water. Repeat three times. You should now have a full bowl of paper pulp. Stir in the wheat starch.

3 Stir the pulp with your hands and, with a sponge, wet the mesh screen of the mould. Holding the mould with the screen uppermost, lower into the pulp at the back of the bowl. In one smooth, level movement, take the mould to the bottom of the bowl and up at the front, lifting the mould completely out of the water. Allow excess water to drain off.

4 Turn the mould over, placing its front edge at the front edge of the couching mound. Roll the mould onto the mound, pressing firmly, especially at the edges.

5 Roll the mould back, holding down its near edge firmly. The wet paper will be transferred onto the kitchen cloth. Carefully cover with another cloth.

6 Repeat from step 2, this time using the old book to make pulp and adding to the pulp that is left over. Try adding different seeds or grasses, too. Then repeat using the old newspapers, then the craft paper (you are working from the palest colour paper to the darkest), to make a stack of writing paper (each sheet within two kitchen cloths) with a subtle colour graduation. If you wish to make more than 10 sheets of paper, add another tablespoon of wheat starch to the pulp mix.

7

8

7 To press and dry the paper, lay a wooden board on the floor, covered with two dry newspapers. Carefully place the sheets of paper, still in the kitchen cloths, onto the newspaper. Lay two more dry newspapers on top, then another wooden board. Stand on the board for a minute or so.

8 Remove the newspapers and, with the paper still in the kitchen cloths, leave to dry either on flat, dry newspapers or by carefully pegging to a washing line. When completely dry, carefully peel the paper away from the cloths.

Papier mâché

Literally meaning 'chewed-up paper', papier mâché is inexpensive and easy to work with, light yet strong and tough yet delicate. Its versatility has made it popular all over the world, for brightly coloured folk art, detailed decorative mouldings, furniture of all kinds and, today, sophisticated accessories.

Paper was invented in China in the second century AD, and papier mâché inevitably followed soon after – being a good way of re-using a commodity that was limited and expensive. It was also exceptionally strong for its light weight and, toughened with lacquer, was used by the ancient Chinese for making war helmets, among other things. The craft eventually spread to Samarkand and Morocco, and from there, by the 10th century, to Spain, France, Germany, Italy, Persia and India.

The first Europeans to see the value of papier mâché were the French, who used it to make items such as snuff boxes and cups, and to imitate plaster and stucco, though only on a relatively small scale. But it was enthusiastically taken up in England, where mashed paper or sheets of paper pasted together were moulded, baked and often varnished ('japanned') to form light, inexpensive decorative mouldings that could be sawn and screwed just like wood.

By the 1770s, papier mâché manufacturing was one of the most important trades in the midlands of Britain, producing not just mouldings but trays, chairs, tables, lamp stands, sconces, coach panels, bookcases, screens, candlesticks, bedsteads and all sorts of other domestic items. These usually had a black background and intricately painted floral decoration, and were sometimes gilded and inlaid with mother-of-pearl. In France and Germany, too, papier mâché furniture had by now become popular, and in all three countries, makers were experimenting with the medium, creating extraordinary items, including a fully functioning watch and a village of ten prefabricated papier mâché houses. Papier mâché was also practised in America, Russia and Scandinavia – in Norway in 1793, for example, an entire church was built from papier mâché and stood for 37 years.

Papier mâché's heyday in Europe lasted about a century, but by the 1870s its popularity was decreasing, its novelty having worn off and its designs no longer considered sophisticated, but garish and crude. Although mass production came to an end, there was, however, still a demand for hand-made papier mâché used for traditional folk craft, such as puppet shows (Punch and Judy in Britain, Pulcinella in Italy, for example) and figures or masks in processions. In fact, it is in such ancient, individual ways that papier mâché lives on around the world – in the form of Japanese toys; Indian painted vases, boxes, lampshades, bangles, cups and bowls; and Mexican dolls, *piñatas* (containers holding sweets and small toys), masks and figures. Such tradition and ancient symbolism, married with bright colours and intricate patterning, are often found in papier mâché. Modern craftspeople, however, are just as likely to use 21st-century imagery, subtle colours and sophisticated, minimal patterns to explore this medium's endlessly inventive potential.

Making this project may bring back childhood memories, but this simple bowl with its delicate decoration is perfectly grown-up, very subtle and sophisticated.

Leaf bowl

you will need

- Newspapers
- Protective gloves (if you are sensitive to glue)
- Wallpaper paste
- Mixing bowl
- Mixing spoon
- PVA glue
- Clingfilm
- Glass bowl of the same shape and size as the one you wish to make
- At least 6 sheets of A4 recycled paper
- Paintbrush
- 3–4 sheets of A4 hand-made paper
- Skeleton leaves (quantity will depend on the size of your bowl and your chosen design)

While vivid shades and bold patterns can be highly effective in papier mâché, there is much to be gained from exploring a contemporary look that plays on form and texture rather than just colour. The key to the charm of this project is to choose a mould in a lovely shape, then it is simply a question of building up layers until you have a form that appears fragile, but is actually rather strong. Scatter on dried leaves, flowers, petals, ferns or similar, and use for whatever purpose you like, whether display, storage or simple ornament.

how to make: **Leaf bowl**

1 Cover your work surface with newspaper. Wearing the gloves (if necessary), mix up the wallpaper paste in a bowl, three parts paste to one part PVA glue. With the clingfilm, carefully cover the entire bowl that you will use as a mould.

2 Tear the recycled paper into strips measuring 2 x 6cm. Using the paintbrush, paste the strips in slightly overlapping rows on the inside of the bowl, smoothing down the strips as you go. Where the paper reaches the rim, leave the edge slightly rough and uneven to complement the natural look of this project. Allow to dry.

3 Paste a second layer of strips, this time in the opposite direction to the first. Allow to dry. Continue until you have applied at least six layers, leaving each layer to dry individually. When the final layer is dry, carefully remove the papier mâché bowl from the mould.

4 Tear up the hand-made paper and, using the PVA glue, cover the inside and outside of the papier mâché bowl.

5 Using the PVA glue, decorate the inside of the bowl with skeleton leaves, placed randomly.

6 Set the bowl aside, so that the glue has a chance to dry completely before use.

how many layers?
The more layers of paper you apply, the stronger the bowl will be. If you decide to make a bigger bowl, you will need to apply more layers, so that it is strong enough to support its own weight.

how

1 Foll
the
to make

2 Co
the
in a bo
the recy

3 Pas
insi
as you
this tim
to dry.
as the f

4 If y
squ
box with
recycled

5 To
the
togethe
out thre
Adjust t
rectangl
rectangl

6 Tea
glue
rim by a
so it doe
box, tak
Using th
with the

7 Care
recy

8 Cut
Glue
and tape
pad to th

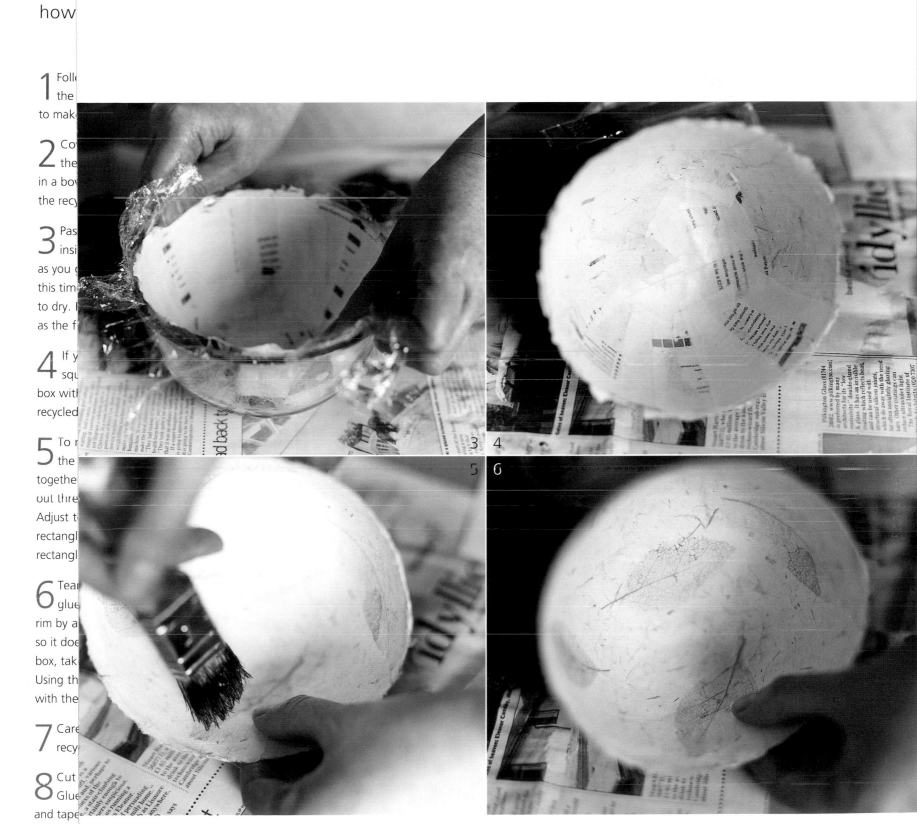

3

4

5

6

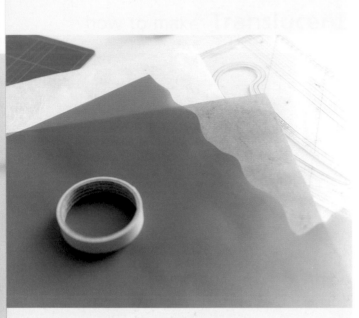

Bold stripes and intriguing colours give these fabulous covered books an air of utter sophistication. The look is modern yet classic, and the project itself combines practicality with decorative effect.

Book covers

you will need

- Selection of different papers in a variety of colours, textures and weights (you will need about 9 different A3 sheets to cover an A4 book)
- Ruler
- Hardback notebook or photograph album
- Double-sided tape
- Spray adhesive
- Craft knife
- Clear sticky-back plastic

Bound blank paper is always useful, whether for photograph albums or sketch books, recipe holders or notebooks. The next step is to create a cover that will protect the books and look appealing, too. This project takes a simple idea – stripes – and gives it a clever twist by using different widths and unusual colour combinations. The hand-torn edges of each stripe demonstrate the textural nature of the paper itself, and give the covers a fuss-free, hand-made look. The result is something that is almost too good to use.

1

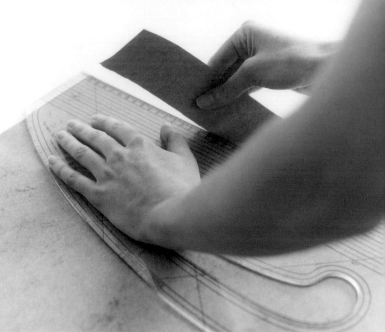

2

3

4

5

6

how to make:
Book covers

1 Arrange your papers so that you can picture them as strips of varying widths, ensuring that the final selection is balanced and pleasing, with wide strips in pale or neutral colours and thinner strips of more intense colour.

2 Tear the strips by holding a ruler level to the edge of the paper. You may wish to measure the strip first so that it is the same width all the way down. Holding it firmly with one hand, use the other to tear the paper down the line of the ruler carefully, creating a pleasing rough edge. Ensure that the strips are about 10cm longer than your book, both at the top and the bottom.

3 Start by covering the book at the spine. Place a length of double-sided tape down the spine and spray a strip of paper, wide enough to overlap the front and back of the book, with spray adhesive. Fix the strip to the spine and, with the book closed, fold the paper round the sides. Do not worry if the paper starts to peel away a little – it can be secured later. Cut four incisions into the excess paper, two at the top and two at the bottom, where the spine and the covers meet. Open the book flat, fold over the paper and fix it to the inside covers of the book with double-sided tape. You should now be left with a 'tongue' the same width as the spine. Trim this until it is about 4cm long and carefully tuck it down into the gap where the pages and the cover separate when the book is opened.

4 Cover the rest of the book by slightly overlapping successive strips of paper, working from the spine to the edge. Ensure that each strip is straight. Fix strips of double-sided tape on the inside covers, along the top and bottom edges. Then fold over the ends of the strips and secure them on the inside of the cover.

5 For the last lengths on the outside edges of the book, position two wide strips on the front and back of the cover. Use a craft knife to cut across the corner of the excess paper, so that when it is folded over the edges, it makes neat, mitred corners.

6 Firmly fold over the edges of the paper and crease. Secure on the inside cover with double-sided tape.

7 Cut a piece of clear sticky-back plastic large enough to wrap around the book and with enough excess to fold over the edges. Very carefully score a strip of the backing

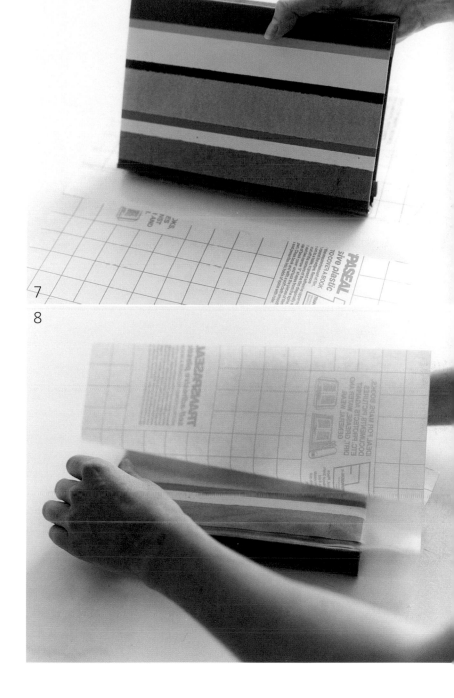

paper from the centre, exposing the sticky plastic. Leave the plastic on a flat surface and place down the spine of the closed book so that it adheres. Cut and tuck the plastic around the spine as with the paper in step 3.

8 Gently peel away the backing paper, smoothing the plastic onto the book. When all the backing paper has been peeled off, cut a mitred corner and fold the plastic over the edges. To tidy the inside cover of the book, cut a rectangle from one of the thicker papers, small enough to fit within the edges of the cover, but large enough to cover the rough edges of the paper and plastic. Attach this using strips of double-sided tape along all four edges.

six

CERAMICS & GLASS

Ceramic painting

Since Iron Age man first shaped clay into small figures of animals, we have been fascinated by our ability to create pottery from the earth. And while function has frequently been the foremost consideration, surface decoration has been intrinsic to the craft, from ancient times to the present day.

The discovery of clay's potential occurred at various times around the world, from Africa to South America, Europe to the Far East. One of the first civilizations to develop a sophisticated ceramic tradition was that of Ancient Greece, where elegant jars, urns, amphorae, bowls and jugs were part of ceremonial and everyday life. Decoration was initially in abstract, geometric patterns, but later, narrative scenes were painted in a glossy black slip, sometimes scratched through with a pointed implement (the *sgraffito* technique). The Romans inherited Greek techniques and spread them through the Empire, commonly embellishing red earthenware forms with raised patterns and a fine slip.

When the Roman Empire fell, ceramic techniques died away in Europe, but in China the industry had become highly sophisticated. High-firing kilns allowed a wide range of glazes, but decoration was not an end in itself, going hand in hand with perfection of form. And when porcelain was discovered during the Tang dynasty (618–906), craftsmen were given a supremely fine material with which to show off their skill. The resulting use of sensuous glazes applied to simple shapes was subtle and utterly beautiful.

Throughout early Medieval Europe much pottery was utilitarian and decorated minimally, if at all. In the Near East, however, new skills of lead and tin glazing and lustre decoration had evolved, which reached a peak in 13th-century Spain. The Italian nobility loved this work, which featured bright, clear colours on a white background, and Italian potters took it up to such an extent that by the 15th century their *majolica* ware dominated the European market.

Trade with the Far East in the 17th century introduced Europeans to the finesse of Chinese ceramics, which now featured a new style – blue and white paintings of naturalistic scenes. It became enormously popular in the West and helped raise the quality of European ceramics in general as German, French and English makers realized just how great the demand could be for good-quality work. Thus were established the great factories of Meissen, Sèvres, Limoges, Wedgwood and Spode.

Despite the high standards of these manufacturers, the production of ceramics became increasingly industrialized, and it was not until the middle of the 19th century that the Arts and Crafts movement urged a return to the craftsman who made and decorated his own work. Thereafter, the studio movement spread through Europe and America, and individual potters explored (again) the influences of the Far East, considered form versus function and began to regard pottery as sculpture. Studio pottery grew and grew, gaining influence and experimenting ever more daringly, so that the styles we see today, which build on the techniques of the past but also break new ground, could scarcely be more diverse and intriguing.

Flowers look beautiful in a sleek-looking modern white vase, and the fresh simplicity of this design would offset any floral arrangement wonderfully.

Painted vase

you will need

- White vase with a smooth (either matt or shiny) glazed surface
- Washing-up liquid
- Newspapers
- Overalls, apron or an old shirt
- White tile or an old piece of white ceramic
- Flat, soft watercolour paintbrushes
- Ceramic paints in your choice of colours (this project used blue and turquoise)
- Old plate to mix colours on
- Scissors
- Masking tape
- Ruler
- White spirit
- Cotton buds
- Large sheet of watercolour paper and acrylic paints (optional)
- Paper kitchen towels (optional)
- Ceramic painting pens (optional)

Painted pottery can be crude and unsophisticated, but with care it can just as easily be delicate and subtle, as shown by this project, which takes as its starting point a plain vase in a delightfully considered shape. Don't be taken in by the apparent simplicity of the painting, however – though it is not overly difficult to achieve this look, it really is well worth practising first on some unwanted pieces of white china in order to perfect exactly the watery, brushed-on effect that makes this design so appealing.

how to make: Painted vase

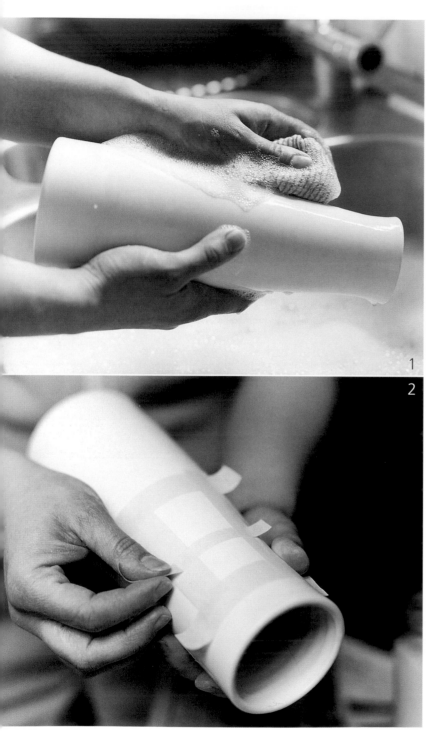

1 Wash the vase in hot soapy water. Dry thoroughly. Cover your working area with newspapers. Wearing overalls, an apron or an old shirt, practise painting on a tile or old piece of ceramic (mixing colours on a plate).

2 Cut five strips of masking tape, each about 10cm long, and apply two strips vertically and three strips horizontally to the vase, to form two rectangles in its centre. Rub over the tape so the paint cannot seep underneath.

3 Stir the ceramic paints (do not shake, as this can create air bubbles). Paint onto the vase, inside the masked-off areas, with as few strokes as possible. Aim to create flat blocks of colour with just one layer, working quickly and covering the area with one or two brushes of paint. After painting, wash the brush immediately in hot, soapy water.

4 Leave to dry for a few minutes until the paint is tacky, then carefully remove the masking tape.

5 Clean untidy edges with white spirit and a cotton bud. Leave to dry for 24 hours in a dust-free place.

6 Follow the manufacturer's instructions to finish the pot in the oven. Ensure the room is ventilated and that no children or pets are around. (Before washing the vase in a dishwasher, check the paint manufacturer's guidelines.)

professional painting

Before painting, you may wish to practise on a sheet of watercolour paper, using ordinary acrylic paint. On three-dimensional objects, paint can seep to the bottom. Collect it with the tip of a dry, clean, flat brush.

To apply watery washes, contain the paint within a masked-off area and apply a small amount at a time. If the colour looks thin, apply another layer; if it is too thick, dab with a kitchen towel. You could experiment with freehand painting and ceramic painting pens.

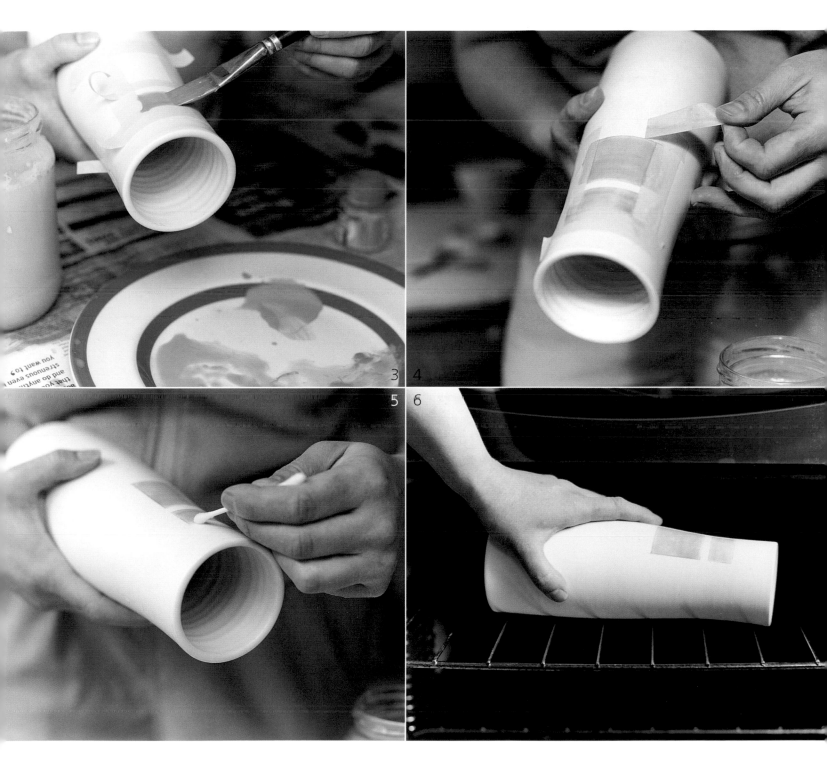

3 4

5 6

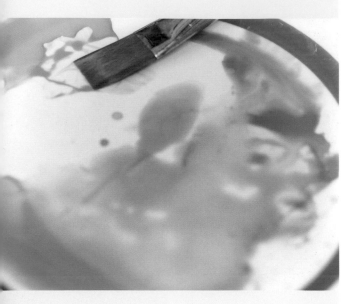

Take your time over a cup of tea or coffee with a set of adorable cups and saucers hand-painted in shades that perfectly complement your interior décor.

Cup and saucer

This project explores the pleasant possibilities of soft, easy-going colours that are layered onto each other for an unusual effect. Strong squares and rectangles create a graphic, dynamic pattern that is contemporary without being harsh, and the watered-down paints soften the look to create a painterly effect that nicely complements the crisp, clean forms of the cup and saucer themselves. This is ceramic decoration at its most mature and subtle, though in itself the process could hardly be more straightforward.

you will need

- White cup and saucer with a smooth (either matt or shiny) glazed surface
- Washing-up liquid
- Newspapers
- Overalls, apron or an old shirt
- White tile or an old piece of white ceramic
- Flat, soft watercolour paintbrushes
- Non-toxic ceramic paints in your choice of colours (this project used two shades of blue and one of green)
- Old plate to mix colours on
- Scissors
- Masking tape
- Ruler
- White spirit
- Cotton buds

Glass painting

Sandblasted or stained, acid-etched or relief-moulded, engraved or enamelled, glass can be decorated in innumerable ways. Most of these techniques date back to the days of the ancient Romans, the first glass experts, but modern interpretations give new life to a traditional and timelessly beautiful craft.

The identity of the people who first discovered how to work glass is a mystery, but we do know that the ancient Egyptians became adept at producing brightly coloured, moulded glass items that were considered a great luxury. The Romans used glass extensively, too, and when the technique of glassblowing was discovered (in the first or second century BC), the art flourished. Glassworks were established from Syria to Brittany for objects ordinary and ornate, many of which were cut, engraved, painted, moulded or gilded.

When the Roman Empire collapsed, the glass industry declined, but Byzantine and then Islamic glass continued to flourish, with gilding and enamelling the favourite methods of decoration. In Japan, too, there were skilled glass craftsmen, producing blown glass and delicate pieces in a technique called *cloisonné*, where coloured glass fills tiny gaps between flattened wires.

The idea of using coloured glass to make church window panels appears to have originated in sixth century Constantinople. At first, the glass was stained by adding metallic oxides to the molten glass, but later the stain was painted onto the surface of the glass, and from then on the two techniques were often combined to awe-inspiring effect. Windows became larger and designs more elaborate, and many wonderful church and cathedral windows were produced in the 13th and 14th centuries. At around the same time, Venice emerged as the pre-eminent centre for secular glasswork. In 1291 the Venetian glassworks were moved to the island of Murano, partly as a fire precaution but mostly to control the movement of highly skilled craftsmen. The penalty for revealing their secrets or for leaving the island was death.

Glass decoration, particularly enamelling, gilding and engraving, reached new heights, and Venetian glass was widely exported and imitated. By 1600, however, Venetian techniques (though not necessarily the skills) were common all over Europe, and a glassworks was set up in America in 1609, claiming to be the first industry of the 'New World'.

Techniques continued to develop, and in the late 17th century an Englishman discovered that adding lead to glass made it softer and easier to engrave. This established the lead-crystal glass industry in Britain and then Ireland. The 19th century Art Nouveau movement was a catalyst for another major style of glass decoration, fluid, asymmetrical, elegant and graceful, popularized by the creations of Louis Comfort Tiffany, Émile Gallé and René Lalique.

Glasswork of the early 20th century was more restrained, but a flowering of individualism came with the studio glass movement that began in the 1960s, in which artists worldwide have pioneered interest in glass as a stimulating medium. Contemporary glass, functional or ornamental, is often vigorous and daring, experimenting with a variety of decorative techniques, both old and new.

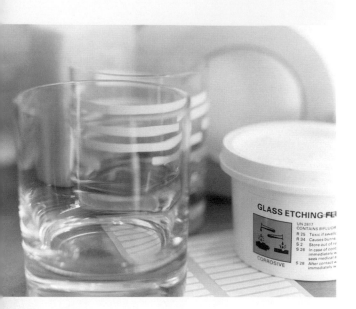

Frosted tumblers make a marvellous point of the contrast between clear and opaque. In this project the pattern is almost like a bar code – strongly linear and appealingly contemporary.

Etched tumbler

you will need

- A clear glass tumbler
- Washing-up liquid
- Newspapers
- Long thin strips of masking tape or stickers
- Overalls, apron or an old shirt
- Rubber or surgical gloves
- Small sponge
- 20ml etching paste
- Plastic bucket
- Half a teaspoon of soda crystals (for safe disposal of etching paste)

Glass etching paste is a wonderfully versatile material with which to experiment, and can be used to paint with either directly or with the aid of a mask or stencil. The trick is to create a pattern that is clear and clean, and here the long, thin lines have a fantastically graphic look that contrasts with the curving form of the glass itself. Of course, you could use all sorts of other stickers as a basis for your design, on tumblers, wine glasses, cups, bowls, plates, vases or any other glass objects you wish. You can make as many tumblers as you like – simply increase the quantities accordingly.

1 2
3 4

how to make:
Etched tumbler

5

1 Ensure that the surface of the tumbler you wish to paint is clean and grease-free by washing in hot, soapy water. Dry thoroughly. If you wish, cover your working area with newspaper.

2 Stick the masking tape or stickers in lines curving around the tumbler. Rub over the tape to ensure that the paste cannot seep underneath.

3 Wearing overalls and the rubber or surgical gloves, use a sponge to cover the tumbler with the etching paste. If you want a completely frosted look, cover it evenly all over. Alternatively, you could create a textural look by dabbing it unevenly and even leaving some areas completely free of paste.

4 Once the tumbler is covered in paste, leave for two minutes, then wash off. To do this you will need to fill a plastic bucket with warm water. Keeping the gloves on, immerse the glass in the water and rinse the paste into the bowl. Use the sponge to wipe off the paste around the stickers.

5 Peel the tape or stickers off the tumbler and wash it thoroughly again, ensuring that you remove all traces of the paste. Leave to dry. (The etching paste is non-toxic and dishwasher-safe.)

safe disposal
You cannot empty the bucket of pasty water down the drain as it is – first you must de-neutralize it properly by adding half a teaspoon of soda crystals. It is then safe to dispose of it.

Mosaic

Combining disciplined design with expression and rhythmic form, mosaics have scarcely changed over the centuries. Floors, walls and furnishings in patterns of stone and glass have the same appealing beauty and practicality for us today as they did for the ancient people of Greece, Rome and the Byzantine Empire.

 The direct roots of mosaic extend back to Ancient Greece, where floors were made from uncut pebbles laid in simple geometric patterns and, later, figurative and floral designs. As its decorative potential became apparent, mosaic became more elaborate, using small cubes of stone, marble and sometimes glass. The gaps between the tesserae were filled with a 'grout' of lime and powdered marble. By the time of the Roman Empire, mosaics had become detailed and realistic, made to such a high standard that they resembled paintings, complete with shadows, highlights and even brushstrokes. They were the usual choice of flooring, and were also used for walls, pavements, vaults and fountains.

It was during the Byzantine era, from the fourth century AD, that mosaic developed as a truly extraordinary craft. In time, glass tesserae came to replace marble and stone almost entirely – their many colours and glittery effect making them an impressive medium with which the early Christian church could depict religious scenes. For about a thousand years, mosaic making was the supreme art form of the Byzantine Empire, from its capital, Constantinople, to the Balkans, Asia Minor, the Middle East, North Africa and the Mediterranean. Technique and artistry combined to create works that were rhythmic and dynamic, their style sparse and flowing, yet powerful in intensity.

Ironically, it was the Renaissance – the flowering of European art and culture – that heralded a decline in mosaic making, as frescos and oil painting came to the fore and attention turned to more realistic ways of depicting man. In Europe, mosaic came to be used for little more than copies of paintings, though in Central America the Conquistadors made inventive mosaics, using natural stones, to cover ritual objects in coloured patterns.

It was not until the early 20th century that mosaic enjoyed a revival, when the Art Nouveau movement rediscovered its potential. It was employed by Gustave Klimt for murals in a Brussels house and used extensively by Spanish designer/architect Antonio Gaudí, whose outdoor mosaic work was hugely imaginative and exuberant, creating sculptural, three-dimensional forms that were entirely unique. Modern artists, including Léger and Bazaine, made use of the medium's strong colours and abstract shapes, while in the 1950s the Mexican muralists Rivera, Siqueiros, Morado and O'Gorman took mosaic into the realm of socialism, covering public buildings with mosaics that told stories of Mexican history.

Both decorative and functional, mosaic is ideally suited to eye-catching patterning and to stylized, powerful imagery. Modern craftspeople revel in its versatility and experiment with its dynamism, using materials that range from 'found' objects to precisely cut smalti. Mosaic is a craft that has changed surprisingly little over the course of centuries, and is still very much alive today.

how to make:
Coloured shelf

1 Sand the piece of plywood or MDF with the sandpaper and block until all the rough edges are smooth and even. This will provide the perfect surface for priming.

2 Wearing surgical gloves and overalls, and working in a well-ventilated area, prime the top and three sides of the board by painting them with the PVA glue (wash the paintbrush immediately afterwards). Leave to dry.

3 Lay down a dust sheet and, wearing safety glasses and a protective mask, cut about a quarter of each colour of the smalti into halves. Hold a tessera with your thumb and finger and place it with the part you want to cut over the blade of the hardie. Bring the hammer down lightly but firmly onto the centre of the tessera. Avoid inhaling dust by not cutting directly under your nose.

4 Still wearing the surgical gloves and overalls, mix the adhesive with the additive and water in a bucket or bowl, following the manufacturer's instructions, then place a small amount onto a trowel and apply to one end of the board. Stick down the tesserae one band of colour at a time, mixing the cut and uncut tiles for interest, but ensuring that they are evenly spaced. Each band is four whole tesserae wide and 12 long.

5 When the top is complete, stick the tesserae around the edges, in corresponding colours to the design on the top. Leave to dry for 24 hours.

6 Remove any protruding adhesive from between the tesserae with a bradawl or prodding tool. Go carefully, so as not to damage the surrounding tesserae. Clean with a damp sponge. When dry, polish with a soft, dry cloth to achieve a shine.

7 Hang the shelf on the wall, using the brackets. If you wish, you could place a sheet of glass on top, using the rubber stoppers as a buffer between the mosaic and the glass.

7

storing materials
When storing tesserae, it is best to make them easily identifiable, so glass or transparent containers are ideal for loose cubes and clearly labelled boxes work well for flat sheets. All adhesives, cements and additives are best stored in a cool, dark place.

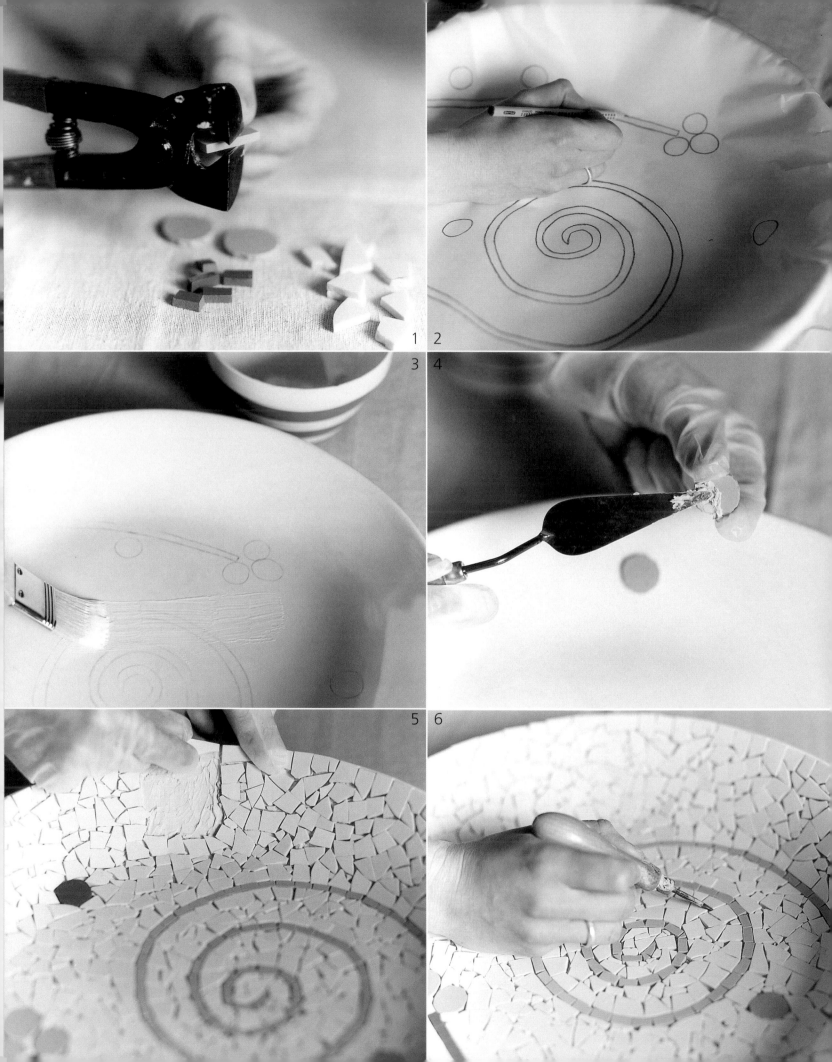

how to make:
Decorative bowl

1 Lay down a dust sheet and, wearing safety glasses, start to cut the mosaic tesserae using the nippers (cut a few at this stage and then more as you need them). Hold the nippers in one hand, towards the bottom of the handle, and a tessera in the other. Place the tessera face up between the cutting edges of the nippers and apply firm pressure. Cut a few of the chocolate brown and beige tesserae into eighths for the outlines, a few of the white tesserae into random shapes for the background, and a few of the pink and chocolate brown tesserae into circles. To do this, nip off the corners and slowly 'nibble' all the way around the tile in order to produce a smooth, round shape.

2 Trace the design on page 325 onto a piece of tracing paper, turn over and draw the outlines again, then place the paper into the bowl and trace the design onto it (you may need to enlarge or reduce it on a photocopier).

3 Wearing the surgical gloves and overalls, and working in a well-ventilated area, apply a coat of PVA glue to the bowl (wash the paintbrush immediately afterwards) to prime it. Allow to dry. Mix the adhesive with the additive and water in a bucket according to the manufacturer's instructions.

4 Place a small amount of adhesive onto a palette knife and apply to the small circles of the design. Stick the circle-shaped tesserae down, then repeat for the stem.

5 Complete the background of the design by applying the adhesive to the bowl, then sticking down the randomly shaped tesserae, ensuring that they are evenly spaced. Start by outlining the details you have already completed, then fill in the rest of the background. Leave to dry for 24 hours.

6 Remove any protruding adhesive from between the tesserae using the bradawl. Clean with a sponge.

7 Wearing rubber gloves, mix up the grout with the additive and water, according to the manufacturer's instructions, then smooth on all over the bowl with the float, starting from the centre.

8 Spread the grout outwards and up to the brim of the bowl. Remove any excess with a damp sponge, then clean and polish with a soft, dry cloth. Leave to dry for 24 hours. You may wish to paint the outside of the bowl to match your mosaic or grout colour.

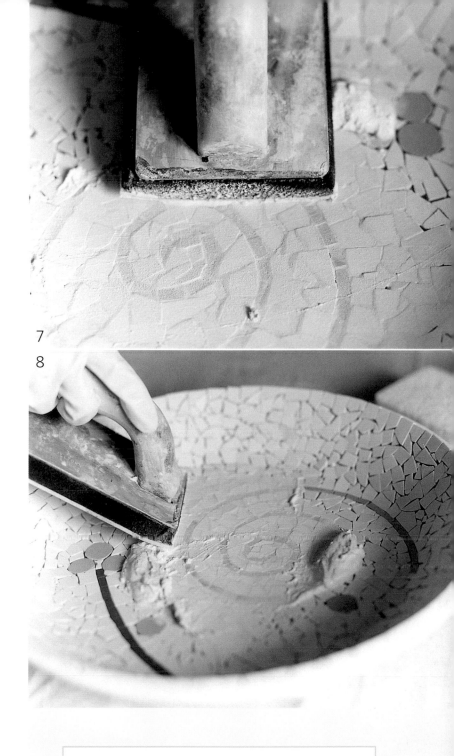

7

8

---

useful equipment
Nippers that have spring-action handles make cutting less arduous. Also, you may find it helpful to use a pair of tweezers to position small tesserae.

seven

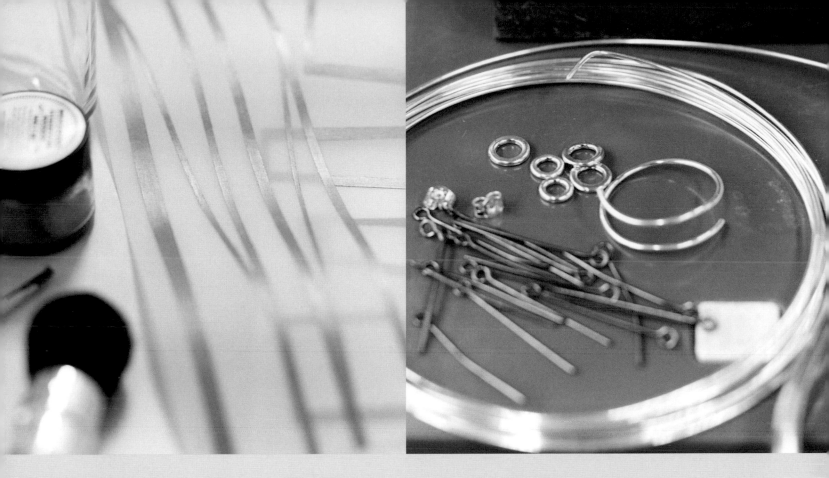

METALWORK

Gilding

The glitter of gold has entranced and delighted man since ancient times, and gold leaf has been employed to decorate objects with religious purpose or simply as a means of displaying power or wealth. Gilding can be subtle and delicate or excessively lavish, but it is always fascinating and alluring.

 While traces of gold have been found in caves used by Palaeolithic man around 40,000BC, the date it was first put to use is open to speculation. It is thought that Egyptian pharaohs and priests began to use gold as an adornment around 3,000BC, linking it to their sun-god, Ra. Eventually they discovered that it was possible to beat the precious metal into very thin sheets and apply it to surfaces as a decoration for religious artefacts. In time, the technique of gilding spread to China and the Greek and Roman Empires, with stunning results – ornaments, items of furniture and even religious buildings shone with the lustre of applied gold.

In the early Middle Ages, gilding was practised in Asia and the Middle East, but it did not return to Europe until the 14th century, when it became prized for use on icons and other religious works. In 1437, Italian artisan Cennino Cennini published *Il Libro Dell'Arte* (*The Craftsman's Handbook*), which included detailed instructions for carrying out gilding on wood and glass. Not long afterwards, the technique was perfected when artists, including Giotto, Duccio and Masaccio, realized that layers of gesso and a clay solution would seal the wood, prevent the gilding from flaking away and enhance its depth and colour.

By the 17th century, gilding had reached a peak in Europe. It was an essential element in the baroque style, which began as an attempt by the Church to reinforce its authority, but developed into an extravagant means for the upper classes to flaunt their secular wealth. Dazzling and theatrical, baroque furniture and accessories (many of them imported from the Far East) featured heavy carving and gilding, marquetry and inlays. In the 18th century, a less decadent look prevailed, but gilding continued to be popular, used for architectural emphasis on columns, mouldings and other details, and delicate inlays on furniture, light fittings and picture frames. It was at this time that the term *verre eglomisé* was coined for gilding on glass, after the 18th-century painter and frame maker Jean Baptiste Glomy. Other popular verre eglomisé items included mirrors, table tops, clocks and even whole pictures. In America, a folk art version arose – using imitation gold and metal foil, it was known as 'tinsel painting'.

Complex, time-consuming and expensive, today traditional leaf gilding is usually carried out in order to restore antiques, by expert craftsmen who painstakingly recreate its sumptuous effect. But other methods, including creams, pastes and paints, have been developed, and though their appearance is different, the results can be just as effective. The art of gilding may not be widely practised, but it has not died out, and it is possible to use either the centuries-old technique or its newer counterparts to create modern pieces that are vibrant and impressive.

This table centrepiece employs the delightful technique of verre eglomisé. You could use the same process to make a runner for a dining table, a small top for a bedside table, or even a set of coasters.

Table centrepiece

In verre eglomisé, silver leaf is applied to the underside of glass to beautiful effect – its lustrous, ethereal sheen looks as attractive today as it did hundreds of years ago. To give this ancient technique a modern twist, this project uses a sheet of plain glass combined with a bold pattern. Copy this pattern or devise your own; as an alternative you could even use gold, brass or copper leaf. Although applying the delicate leaf can be fiddly, it becomes easier with practice, and the end result is truly satisfying.

you will need

(To make a 40cm square panel with a central image approx 25 x 35cm)

- 40 x 40cm Optiwhite glass panel, 6mm thick
- 60ml methylated spirits (plus extra for cleaning)
- Soft cloth
- Masking tape
- Two gelatine capsules
- 180ml distilled water
- Two bowls
- Measuring jug
- Glass jar
- Mixing spoon
- Paintbrush
- Booklet loose silver leaf (thin)
- Gilder's tip
- Small jar petroleum jelly
- Cotton wool
- Soft brush (or gilder's mop)
- Ruler
- 25ml (approx.) silver lettering enamel

Wax gilt can be used for decorating almost any surface, and comes in various metallic colours. Here it is used on heavyweight tracing paper to make pretty sleeves for glass tealight holders.

Tealight sleeves

Wax gilt is easy to use and creates immediate and impressive results. While familiar in traditional designs, there is no reason why it should not be used in more modern ways – it simply depends on the materials and designs you choose. This project makes the most of the interplay between the semi-transparent tracing paper and the opacity of gilded patterning; flickering candlelight not only emphasizes the contrast, but also enhances the soft sheen of the metal. Create infinite variations on this theme simply by cutting your adhesive film to create any variety of stencil patterns.

you will need

(To make 3–4 sleeves, depending on the size of the tealight holder)
- A3 sheet tracing paper (112gsm)
- Ruler
- Pencil
- Glass tealight holder
- Newsprint (or other clean paper)
- Adhesive film
- Small, flat brush
- 25g wax gilt (copper, gold or silver)
- Small piece of muslin
- Soft brush
- Scalpel
- Cutting mat
- Spray adhesive

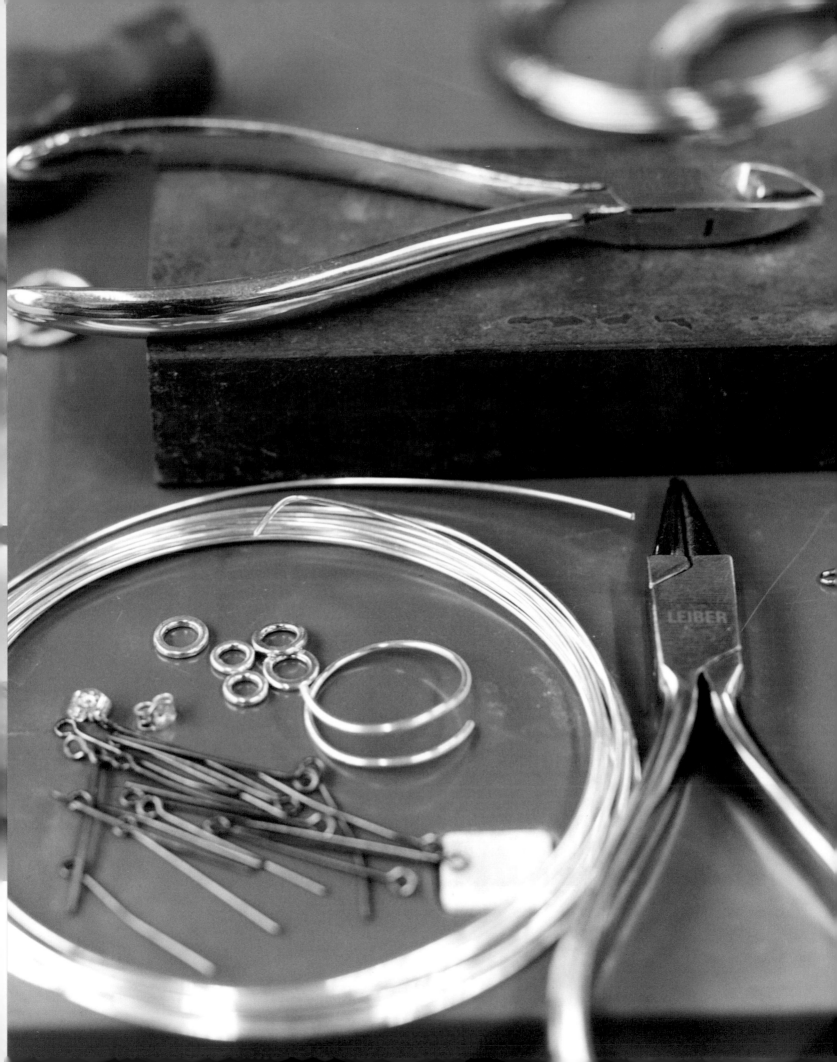

Silverwork

Silver comes second only to gold in terms of the degree to which we treasure it – its colour and brilliance, light weight, resistance to tarnishing and malleability, coupled with its relative scarcity, have made it a prime choice for precious jewellery, ornaments and coins since earliest times.

It is thought that silver was discovered around 6,000 years ago, soon after gold and copper, and that by around 2,000BC the process of smelting to extract the metal from lead was being carried out. The first people to take advantage of silver's special qualities were Mycenean craftsmen, who produced large quantities of dishes and drinking vessels, using techniques that would still be familiar today. Silver has been used for jewellery, decorative objects and coins ever since, and in Medieval Europe it was essential in the creation of chalices, gospel covers and other decorative artefacts for the Christian church. Silver workshops were established in monasteries, and gradually the craft developed in the outside world. Guilds of goldsmiths (the term covered people working in both gold and silver) were set up, and in time the practice of hallmarking was introduced in order to control the purity of the metals. Interestingly, the metalworking techniques described in the 12th century working manual *De Diversis Artibus* have hardly changed at all in the intervening 900 years.

The practice of tea-drinking, which became popular in polite society in the late 17th century, gave new impetus to silver designers, who created entire tea sets in elaborate and sumptuous designs. Silver was highly fashionable, not just for eating and drinking utensils, but also for chandeliers, fireplace accessories, candlesticks and even silver-plated chairs and chests. The abundant use of silver in the Baroque period gave way, in the 18th century, to a more sophisticated look, with designs that were simple, spare and elegant.

It was around this time, however, that the plating trade developed. This, coupled with increased mechanization, eventually led to a deterioration in quality – though of design rather than manufacture – and in the 19th century the most desirable silverwork was antique, or copies of antiques. This was a phenomenon that some silver designers attempted to redress, among them Christopher Dresser, whose minimal design style was an important precursor of Modernism, and C.R. Ashbee, an Arts and Crafts designer whose Guild of Handicraft produced austere but beautiful silverware that was also to become hugely influential for 20th-century silver designers.

Contemporary craftspeople working in silver still battle against the tide of inexpensive, mass-produced products and the desire for cutlery and other utensils that do not require polishing and that can be washed in a dishwasher. Some beautiful work, however, both functional and sculptural, proves how much impact silver can make in the home. And silver jewellery remains as popular as it ever was – whether in the form of solid, cast silver, flat, beaten work or wire, modern silver jewellery is both innovative and wearable, demonstrating without a doubt the desirability of this timeless precious metal.

Silver has been fashionable since ancient times, and when it is used to create a simple, modern design it has a timeless quality that is as desirable now as it was thousands of years ago.

Coil earrings

you will need

- 16cm soft silver wire (plated or real), 1mm thick (it is advisable, however, to buy more wire to allow for experimentation and mistakes)
- Wire cutters
- File
- Round-nosed pliers
- Flat-nosed pliers
- Metal block or surface (textured if possible)
- Hammer (textured if possible)
- Earring butterflies to fit 1mm wire (if you cannot find these, buy a standard pair of butterflies and file down the ends of the wire)

Making your own jewellery is hugely satisfying, especially when you can work with a precious metal without needing to buy expensive and difficult-to-use equipment. These silver earrings, which could be worn either with a casual outfit or as a smart accessory, are intricate and delicate in style, yet not at all fussy or fiddly. With a little practice, making the spirals will become second-nature. The hammered surface on the shiny silver wire is a clever touch that adds textural interest to the dynamic form.

For a Christmas decoration – or indeed any other time of the year – this lovely hanging heart will add a dainty touch to a mantelpiece, window, door frame or shelf and, of course, a Christmas tree.

Hanging heart

While the Slovakian tinkers may not have recognized this modern version of wirework, this project is undoubtedly highly desirable, decorative and appealing. Most obviously a Christmas decoration, it could equally well be used as an informal hanging anywhere in the house, throughout the entire year. Once you have mastered the heart shape, try your hand at creating circles, ovals, squares and even stars – the basic technique is exactly the same and it would be wonderful to make a series of hangings in different shapes and sizes.

you will need

(To make the triple heart hanging in the centre of the picture, right)

- About 300 assorted beads, approximately 275 tiny ones and 25 medium-sized ones (new or taken from old jewellery)
- Small container for holding beads, preferably with compartments
- 100cm of 1mm galvanized tying wire
- Small pliers (with a cutting edge)
- Reel of florist's or 'rose' wire
- One silver headpin
- Heart-shaped bead (or a pear-drop, or any pretty hanging bead)
- Silver thread or coordinating ribbon for hanging

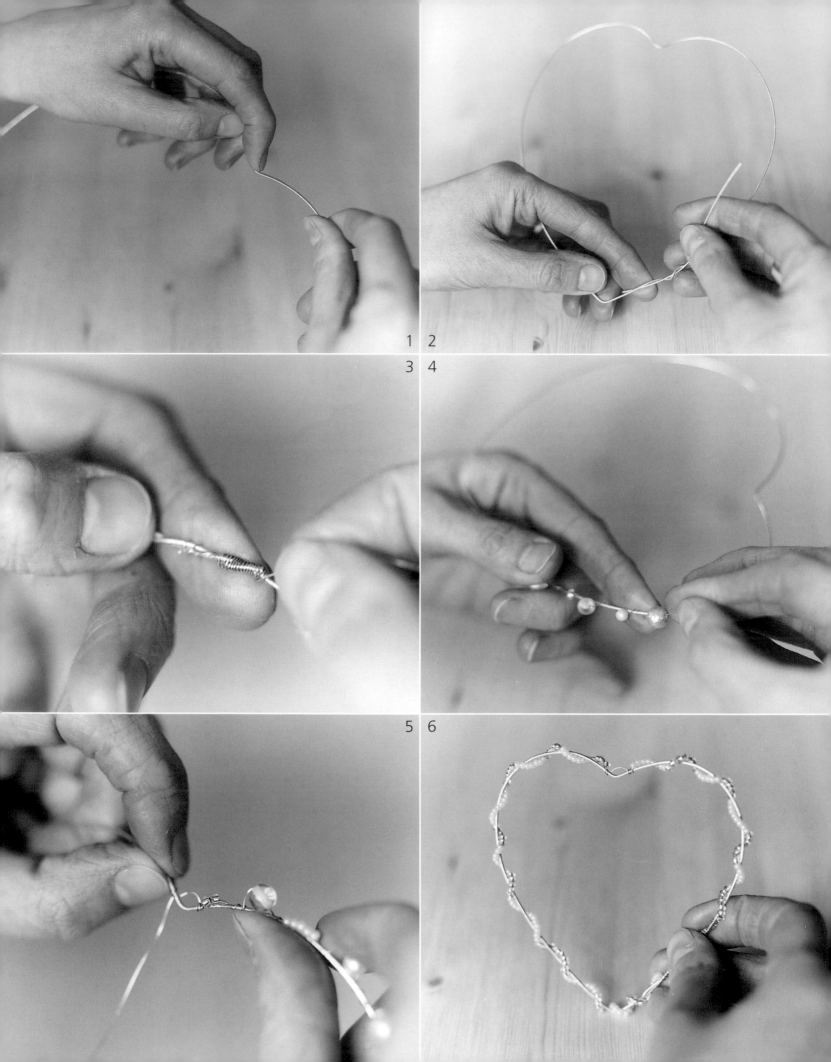

1 2

3 4

5 6

how to make:
Hanging heart

1 Choose a selection of colour-coordinated beads and set aside in a container. Begin by making the largest heart. Cut 50cm of the 1mm wire with the pliers and, using the natural curve of the wire, bend it (with the middle about 3cm from the centre of the length of wire) to form the two arcs that are the top of a heart.

2 Holding firmly, and being very careful, curve both ends down to form a heart. Be firm, but do not make kinks as they will be very difficult to smooth out. When you are happy with the shape, sharply bend the longer end of wire upwards to form the bottom point of the heart. Twist it around the shorter end two or three times to fix in place. Cut the ends and pinch in with pliers. You may need to tease the heart into shape.

3 Cut a length of the florist's wire (about 40–60cm is comfortable to work with) and anchor it by winding tightly around the joining twist of the heart base shape many times, until the ends are covered.

4 Wind the florist's wire around the heart shape and add the beads, alternating sizes and colours, at intervals by threading them on

5 Every time you add a bead, anchor it in place by winding the wire around the base shape twice. When you run out of florist's wire, wind round four or five times and squeeze in the end with pliers. Attach a new length at the same point and continue. When you reach the top of the heart, form a tiny arch with the florist's wire then continue down the other side. Finish by winding the wire around tightly four or five times, then cutting off as close as possible to the base shape and using the pliers to pinch in the end neatly.

6 Make the second heart base shape as in steps 1 and 2, using about 35cm of the 1mm wire. Thread a selection of small beads continuously onto lengths of florist's wire and wind them around the heart shape, attaching and finishing as in steps 3 and 5. Remember to make a small arch at the top with the florist's wire.

7 For the third heart, use 25cm of the florist's wire, threading small beads onto it and then bending it

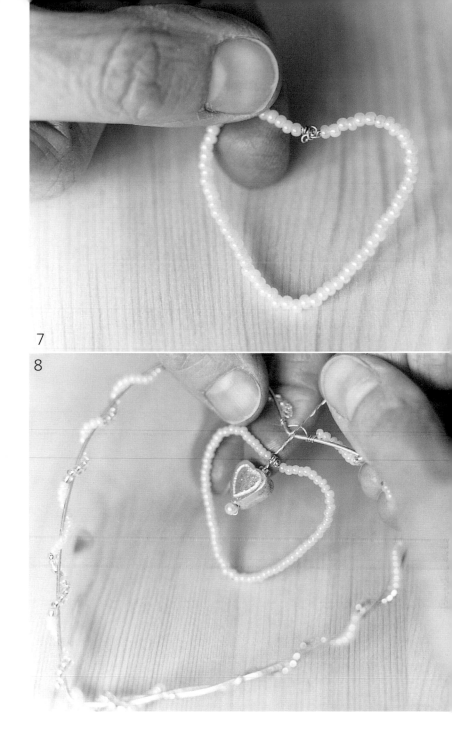

7

8

into a heart shape. Make a small loop at the top with a twist of wire.

8 Thread a bead onto the headpin, then the heart-shaped bead, then another bead. Bend the top of the pin with pliers to form a loop and hang this from the loop at the top of the smallest heart. Use a short length of wire to twist around the centre of all three hearts so that they are loosely linked together. To hang, loop a silver thread or ribbon through the largest heart.

eight

CASTING & MOULDING

How nice it is to make a joy of something as utilitarian as a bar of soap! These tempting examples can – like a block of cheese – be cut into lovely thick slabs when required.

Clear soap block

you will need

(To make one block of soap)
- Mould (a large margarine tub is ideal, as long as it is sturdy enough to withstand the heat of the melted soap)
- Petroleum jelly
- 1.2kg clear melt-and-pour soap base
- Kitchen knife
- Double boiler (or saucepan and heatproof bowl)
- Mixing spoon
- Candy thermometer (optional)
- Mixing bowl
- 8ml liquid soap colourant (this project used orange)
- Measuring spoons
- 12ml essential oil (this project used Sweet Orange)
- Small spritzer bottle containing alcohol (optional)
- Knife, vegetable peeler or damp sponge
- Cheese wire or herb chopper
- Clingfilm

If you can bake a cake, you can make soap just as easily. This straightforward method, known as melt-and-pour, involves nothing more complex than heating gently and pouring the softened mixture into a greased mould. The possibilities of gorgeous colour and delicious scent, however, are endless, and once you have tried once or twice you are bound to want to keep going. Make your soaps in different shapes and sizes, and display them on a window ledge in the bathroom or kitchen so that the light enhances their gorgeous jewel-like qualities.

Plastic design

Since they were first developed in the 19th century, plastics have transformed our lives, surrounding us at home and at work, indoors and out. Essential for industry, plastics have also become adapted for craft use, and today they are valued for the unique properties that give them enormous creative potential.

A plastic is simply a material that in itself is inherently formless, but that can be shaped under heat and pressure – from the Greek word *plastikos*, meaning 'to mould or form'. Natural plastics include amber resin and *gutta percha*, a rubber-like substance from a tropical tree, but today we generally use the word to denote man-made materials such as polythene, acrylic and polyester.

The earliest semi-synthetic plastic was Vulcanite, created in the late-1830s by Charles Goodyear, used for matchstick holders and (among other things) false teeth. As the 19th century went on, mechanization increased and new materials had to be found to replace expensive, hand-crafted ones, such as ivory and horn. Plastics were the answer. In the 1860s, celluloid became the first mass-produced plastic, made into all sorts of items, from dressing table sets to jewellery and cigarette cases. Three decades later casein plastic was invented and then, in 1907, came the biggest breakthrough of all – Bakelite, the first truly synthetic plastic, invented by American Leo Baekeland.

Best-known for its use in radios, Bakelite was actually employed in the manufacture of all sorts of domestic products, and it was at this time that designers really began to appreciate the versatility, cheapness and creative potential of plastics. In the 1920s and '30s, important inventions included polythene, nylon, acrylic, polystyrene and polyurethane, and these materials were used more and more widely, for everyday necessities and luxury items. In the 1940s and '50s, unfortunately, plastic design was not always of the highest quality. Products were often made in huge volume at very low prices, and so developed the common opinion that plastic was cheap and nasty – a poor imitator of other, natural materials.

Plastic came back into favour in the 1960s, when vivid colours, organic shapes and disposable objects were all the rage. But it was in the 1970s that plastics were taken up by craftspeople, as a material that could compete with wood, textiles, even precious metals, in its own right rather than as a poor imitator or inexpensive substitute. Some jewellers, in particular, chose plastic above other materials precisely because it embodied qualities that were the opposite of those associated with gold, silver or gemstones. In Britain, Holland and America in particular, plastic was essential to what has been dubbed 'the new jewellery'. This focused on ideas rather than material values, and emphasized plastic's individual qualities – its ability to be moulded or cast into many different shapes, its light weight, its colouring (either subtle or vivid), and its light-transmitting capabilities. From those experimental beginnings, the use of plastic in craft is now accepted and appreciated – its unique properties ideal for the modern craftsperson who wishes to explore all sorts of unusual possibilities.

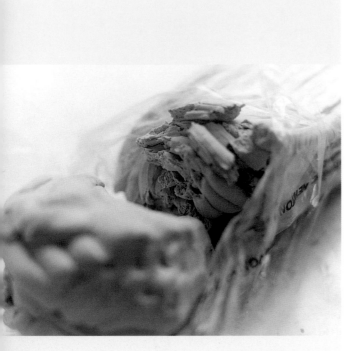

These simple but hardy coasters with their naïve, free design are sharp and modern-looking as well as practical. They will not only protect your furniture from stains but also add contemporary class to your table.

Abstract coasters

you will need

(To make six coasters)
- Ceramic tile
- Block of plasticine (or a ready-made mould)
- Protective mask
- PVC gloves
- 500g general-purpose resin and catalyst
- Small plastic graded cups (similar to measuring jugs) for mixing colours
- Resin paste colours in white, brown and pale blue (in 25g pots)
- Lollipop sticks
- Small amount of detergent
- Old kitchen or craft knife
- Wet and dry sandpaper
- Flocked sticky-back plastic the same size as the tile (optional)

Craftspeople – and especially jewellers – discovered the delights of plastic in the 1970s, and since then it has become increasingly popular as an expressive and intriguing craft material. Resin casting is particularly satisfying as the raw ingredients and the methods involved are relatively straightforward, yet the results can be truly stunning and extremely professional in appearance. These coasters are an easy introduction to the process. Once the basics have been mastered, you could experiment with different colours and patterns, or make your own plasticine moulds in order to create any shape you wish.

how to make: **Abstract coasters**

1

2

1 Choose a ceramic tile in a size and shape you wish to copy, and press the plasticine up evenly around it to create a cavity. Alternatively, you could use a ready-bought mould made of polypropylene. This will be the mould for your coaster. If you wish to make more than one coaster, you will need to make a mould for each.

2 Wearing a mask and gloves, and working in a very well-ventilated room (a good-sized workshop or garage is best), mix around 25ml of resin and 15 drops of catalyst in a plastic graded cup, and add small quantities of one colour of paste. Pour into the plasticine mould so that it is half full and leave to set (this will take around 3–5 hours).

3 Mix the same amount of resin and catalyst again, this time adding a different colour paste. Using a lollipop stick, carefully paint a raised pattern of resin onto the set bottom layer of the tile. Leave to set.

4 Once the raised surface has set, mix another colour and pour in order to fill in the remaining area of the coaster. Leave to set completely for 24 hours.

5 Once hard, remove the coaster from the mould – do not worry if it feels slightly tacky. Soak it in water and detergent.

6 Remove the white layer from the coaster by scraping with an old knife. To finish off, place the coaster on a hard, flat surface and use wet and dry sandpaper on both sides until it is smooth. To protect surfaces, you may wish to stick flocked sticky-back plastic to the back of the coaster.

catalyst quantities
Do not add more catalyst than stated to try to speed things up. This could be dangerous as the catalyst could cause overheating and smoking, and may also result in the piece cracking.

3 4
5 6

These napkin rings look so professional it is hard to believe they are hand made. The combination of clear resin and silver beads is modern and elegant, and would work with almost any table setting.

Napkin rings

you will need

(To make six napkin rings)
- Paper towel tube
- Scissors
- Epoxy putty
- Hot glue gun
- Square of thick, flat card
- Cereal packet
- Sharp craft knife
- Metal ruler
- Masking tape
- Protective mask
- PVC gloves
- 500g silicone rubber
- Electronic scales
- 1kg clear or AM resin and catalyst
- Graded plastic cups (similar to measuring jugs) for mixing
- About 30 small silver beads (large ones will break the surface of the resin)
- Plastic tweezers
- Wet and dry sandpaper
- Metal polish
- Soft cloth

It is difficult to find napkin rings that are eye-catching without being garish, and this project provides the perfect solution. The trickiest part is making the mould – once you've done that, the rest is plain sailing. You could vary the colour of resin or the type of bead for different effects, or even try casting other objects, such as glitter, tiny silk flowers or colourful sweets. Simply ensure that whatever you choose is perfectly dry, non-greasy and not too fragile, and enjoy experimenting to produce unusual and impressive results.

1

2

3

4

5

6

how to make:
Napkin rings

1 Make your ring shape by cutting the desired length from the paper towel tube and coating it in epoxy putty until it is about 1cm thick. Using a hot glue gun, stick it to a square of card to form a flat base.

2 Using an old cereal packet, build a square wall around the tube and tape it together (use a knife and a metal ruler to score the card so that it folds easily). Stick it to the base card with a hot glue gun. Seal the edges with the glue, so that the mould does not leak.

3 Wearing a mask and gloves, and working in a very well ventilated room, mix about 250g silicone rubber according to the manufacturer's instructions (you will need accurate weighing scales). Pour the rubber into the mould, so that it is 1cm higher than the top of the ring, and tap gently to release any air bubbles. Leave for at least 24 hours until set.

4 Ease away all the cardboard and the epoxy putty ring – you will be left with a square of rubber with a ring-shaped cavity in the centre. This is the mould for your napkin ring; it can be re-used many times. (To save time, however, you could make more than one mould at once.)

5 Mix up 25ml of clear resin with 15 drops of catalyst in a graded plastic cup and pour into the mould to a height of about 5mm. Leave to set for 3–5 hours.

6 Have your beads ready and mix more clear resin. Using plastic tweezers, dip a few beads into the resin to coat them, then carefully place in the mould and add a little more resin so that they are just covered. Leave to set again. Repeat as many times as you wish, until the resin is about 5mm from the top of the mould. Finish with a final layer of resin and leave to set completely for 24 hours.

7 Remove the napkin ring from the mould – rubber is flexible so you can be quite forceful if necessary. Finish with wet and dry sandpaper to give a smooth finish.

8 Polish the ring by dipping it in a pool of metal polish and rubbing with a soft cloth to achieve a high shine.

7

8

creating a perfect finish
To give a smooth finish on your epoxy putty 'master' ring (and, therefore, the resin rings themselves), smooth it all over with a damp sponge before use and between mouldings.

sanding the rings
When you are sanding your finished rings, wrap the wet and dry paper around a length of dowelling – this will give you more control when you are working on their curved surfaces.

Acrylic moulding

First used in the First World War as a material for aeroplane windscreens, acrylic has since found many uses both at work and at home. Light, clear, colourful and easy to work with, it has recently become highly appreciated by craftspeople – especially jewellers – who combine skilled workmanship with innovation.

The development of plastics in the late-19th century had far-reaching repercussions. No longer were we obliged to use expensive natural materials that were sometimes in scarce supply, or required time-consuming hand-crafting processes that made them so expensive they were often beyond the reach of ordinary people. Here was a material that could be used for both everyday and upmarket items, which could be moulded, dyed, vacuum-formed, extruded, cut, ground, drilled, polished and cast, made to look like other materials or simply allowed to be itself. Its uses were myriad, from false teeth and dressing table sets in the early days to computer casing and boat hulls today.

Of all the types of plastic in existence, one of the most important is acrylic or, to give it its full name, polymethyl methacrylate, which was produced by the British company ICI in 1936. It is a fully synthetic thermoplastic, which means that it will soften every time heat is applied and can therefore be reformed over and over again. (The other type of plastic is thermosetting, which will soften when heated and then set permanently into its moulded shape when cooled.) Due to its light weight, clarity and shatter-resistant properties, acrylic was first put to use in the form of protective screens, and especially aircraft canopies, during the First World War. It was later used for light fittings,

and then signage – where its ability to take different colours made it an ideal material in the growing corporate identity industry. It was not long before it had become a sophisticated product with a variety of uses, often replacing glass, wood or metal in domestic or commercial environments, and available in a range of thicknesses, colours, tints and surface effects.

In craft work, acrylic figures most predominantly in jewellery, a field that has accepted the use of plastics since the 1920s, when manufacturers first began to make beads, pins and bangles in cast synthetic resins. Something of a novelty at first, plastic gained ground when fashion designer Coco Chanel produced a range of costume jewellery, and thrived during the American depression of the 1930s. In the early 1940s, 'lucky' bracelets were made from the scraps of acrylic left over from the making of fighter plane windscreens, and carved acrylic was used instead of rock crystal, wartime shortages having given costume jewellery another boost.

More creative, rather than imitative, work with acrylic began in the early 1970s, when jewellers discovered how suitable it could be for their work. Among the acrylic pioneers were Claus Bury, Gijs Bakker, Caroline Broadhead and Susanna Heron. Their work paved the way for a new generation of craftspeople who have also found that acrylic is an ideal material with which to introduce innovative ideas, break with past traditions and combine practicality with refinement and vigour with flair.

It is surprising that acrylic is so rarely used as a medium for popular craft. It is light, colourful and easy to work with, and – as can be seen here – wonderfully striking.

Pendant necklace

you will need

(To make one pendant)

- Piece of wet and dry emery paper, 320 grade
- Piece of plate glass or other suitable flat surface
- One piece 4mm-thick clear acrylic sheet, measuring 5cm square. Do not remove the protective paper
- One piece 3mm-thick red fluorescent acrylic sheet, measuring 4 x 4.5cm. Do not remove the protective paper
- File
- Ruler
- Pen
- Upright drill with a sharp, 4mm bit
- Vice
- Protective goggles
- Paraffin
- Fine paintbrush
- Spare 3mm-thick acrylic sheet (any colour) to practise on
- Length of satin or elastic cord, or suede or leather thong

(If you wish to dye your acrylic, see page 319 for equipment)

What could be more satisfying than to transform something that appears to be little more than a waste product into a beautiful pendant necklace? Small scraps of sheet acrylic, in a variety of colours or dyed to a shade of your choice, are easily cut into interesting shapes and drilled (with an ordinary household drill) to produce lovely patterns. The effect of two or more pieces layered onto each other adds another dimension of interest, while the finishing touch is the textural contrast of a satin ribbon or suede thong.

1   2

3   4

how to make:
Pendant necklace

1 Wet the emery paper and place it on the glass (on a flat surface). Rub one edge of one of the pieces of acrylic up and down on the emery paper until it is smooth and matt. Repeat for all edges, then sand the other piece of acrylic, too. File the sharp corners off both pieces.

2 For each of the pieces of acrylic, find the centre of the top edge, and mark 6mm down from this, on the protective paper. Place the bit in the drill and one piece of acrylic in the vice. Wearing protective goggles, and using the paraffin (painted onto the bit) as a lubricant to stop the drill getting too hot, drill on a medium speed all the way through the acrylic at the marked point. Repeat for the other piece of acrylic.

3 On the smaller piece, mark a pattern of random dots. Put a spare piece of acrylic in the vice and practise drilling halfway through. Discard. When you feel confident, place the marked acrylic in the vice and drill halfway through each dot. Remove the protective paper from both pieces.

4 If you wish, you can now dye the clear acrylic. Wearing overalls and rubber gloves, dilute the dye as little as possible in a jug, adding a little washing-up liquid, and bring to the boil in a pan. Hook the wire or string through the hole in the acrylic and immerse in the water. Agitate for five minutes; longer if you want a stronger colour. Remove and, still wearing the overalls and rubber gloves, rinse in warm, soapy water and leave to dry on newspaper.

5 Thread the two pieces of acrylic together with the cord or thong, making sure that you keep the drilled pattern on the inside of the top piece. Then tie the ends together securely at the length you require for your necklace.

5

to dye the pendant, you will need:
- Overalls, apron or an old shirt
- Rubber gloves
- Hot water fabric dye (this project used red)
- Washing-up liquid
- Jug or bowl
- Mixing spoon
- Saucepan
- Short length of coated garden wire or string
- Newspaper

Because acrylic can be moulded so easily, it is perfect for making colourful bangles. Wear just one for subtle impact, or several in a variety of colours.

Simple bangle

you will need

(To make one bangle)
- Piece of wet and dry emery paper, 320 grade
- Piece of plate glass or other suitable flat surface
- Piece of 4mm-thick clear acrylic sheet measuring 2.5 x 22cm. Do not remove the protective paper
- File
- Pen
- Ruler
- Upright drill with a sharp, 4mm bit
- Vice
- Protective goggles
- Paraffin
- Fine paintbrush
- Some spare pieces of scrap acrylic
- Baking tray
- Baking parchment
- Heatproof gloves (old, thick leather gloves are ideal)
- Glass jar, approx 6mm in diameter
- One or two 50cm lengths of ribbon or leather thong

(If you wish to dye your acrylic, see page 323 for equipment)

Acrylic has been a medium of experimentation for cutting-edge professional jewellery makers since the 1970s. It is less often used in a domestic context, however, despite its versatility, practicality and attractive appearance. But now it is time to discover the many wonderful qualities of this modern material. These acrylic bangles really could not be simpler to make – in a variety of colours, widths and thicknesses. You could keep them completely plain and simple, or drill them in several places so as to thread a ribbon through for added decorative interest.

1 2
3 4

how to make:
Simple bangle

Preheat your oven to 140–180°C (gas mark 1–4)

1 Wet the emery paper and place it on the glass. Rub one edge of the acrylic on the emery paper until it is smooth and matt. Repeat for all edges. File the corners.

2 Find the centre of the acrylic and, with a pen, mark 6mm either side of it (in the centre of the width) on the protective paper. Then mark 6mm either side of those points, and 6mm and 12mm in from each end. Place the bit in the drill and the acrylic in the vice. Wearing protective goggles, and using the paraffin (painted onto the bit) as a lubricant, drill on a medium speed right through the acrylic at the marked points. Remove the protective paper from both sides.

3 To test the oven temperature, remove the protective paper from a piece of scrap acrylic and place on a baking tray lined with parchment, then leave in the oven for 10–15 minutes. Remove, with the leather gloves – it should have become floppy. When you have found the correct temperature, place your drilled acrylic on the tray (remove the paper first) and leave in the oven for 10–15 minutes. Remove and, wearing the gloves, wrap it around the glass jar and hold it there to cool. Repeat this if necessary.

4 To dye the bangle, wear overalls and gloves and dilute the dye in a mixing jug, adding a little washing-up liquid. Bring to the boil in a pan. Hook the wire or string through a hole in the bangle and immerse in the water. Agitate for about five minutes. Remove, rinse in warm, soapy water and leave to dry on newspaper. If the bangle opens, return to the oven and repeat the bending process.

5 Finally, thread the ribbon or leather through the holes in the bangle and tie securely.

5

to dye the bangle, you will need:
- Overalls, apron or an old shirt
- Rubber gloves
- Hot water fabric dye (this project used red)
- Washing-up liquid
- Jug or bowl
- Mixing spoon
- Saucepan
- Short length of coated garden wire or string
- Newspaper

Templates

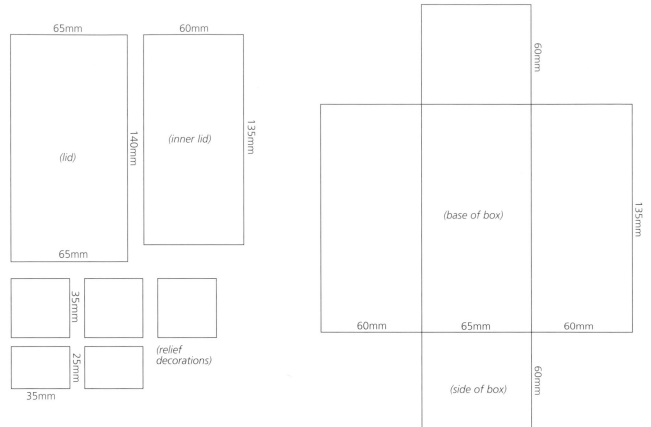

65mm

60mm

(lid)

140mm

65mm

(inner lid)

135mm

60mm

35mm

35mm

25mm

(relief decorations)

60mm

(base of box)

135mm

60mm 65mm 60mm

(side of box)

60mm

Papier mâché:
Jewellery box
pages 214–217

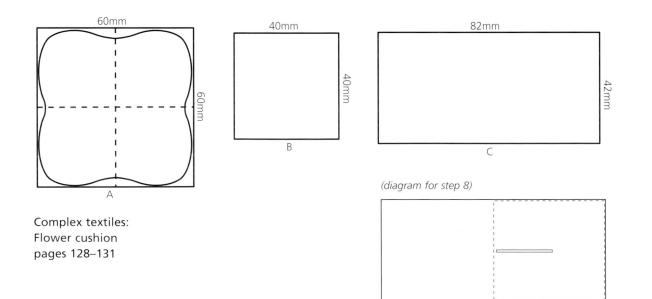

60mm

60mm

A

40mm

40mm

B

82mm

42mm

C

(diagram for step 8)

C

Complex textiles:
Flower cushion
pages 128–131

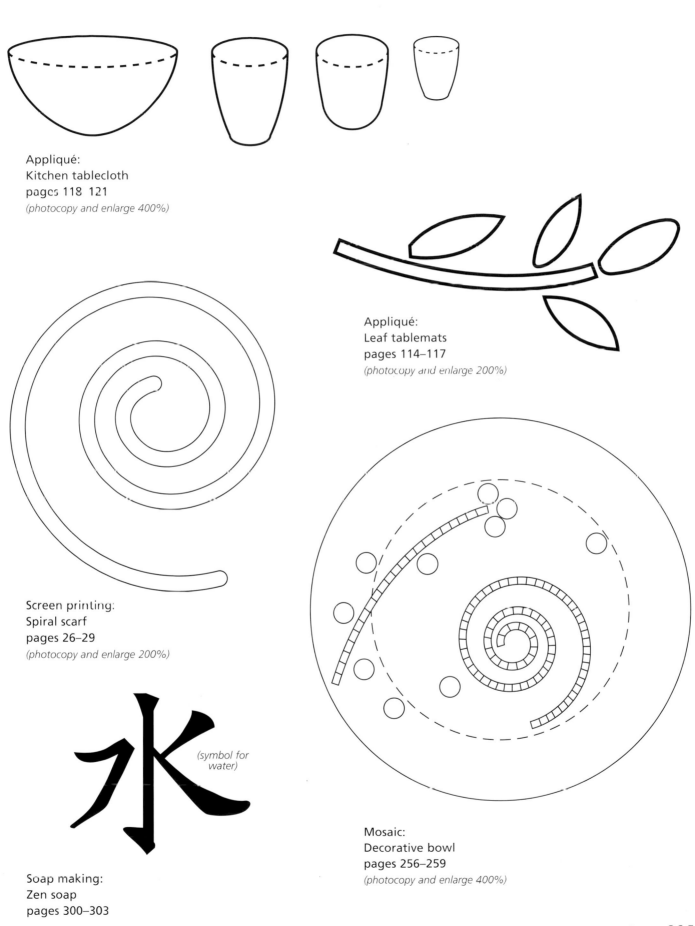

Appliqué:
Kitchen tablecloth
pages 118 121
(photocopy and enlarge 400%)

Appliqué:
Leaf tablemats
pages 114–117
(photocopy and enlarge 200%)

Screen printing:
Spiral scarf
pages 26–29
(photocopy and enlarge 200%)

(symbol for water)

Soap making:
Zen soap
pages 300–303

Mosaic:
Decorative bowl
pages 256–259
(photocopy and enlarge 400%)

45 cm

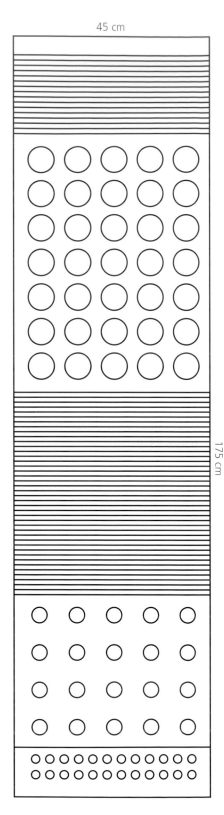

175 cm

Silk painting:
Abstract scarf
pages 46–49
(photocopy and enlarge 800%)

110 cm

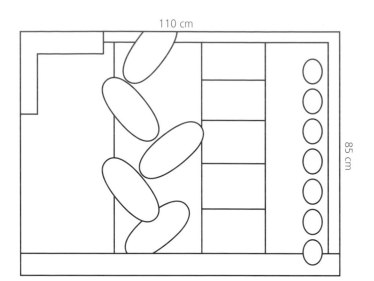

85 cm

Silk painting:
Wall hanging
pages 42–45
(photocopy and enlarge 1000%)

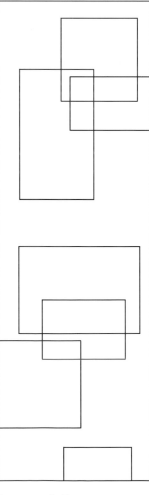

Screen printing:
Wall hanging
pages 22–25
(photocopy and enlarge 1250%)

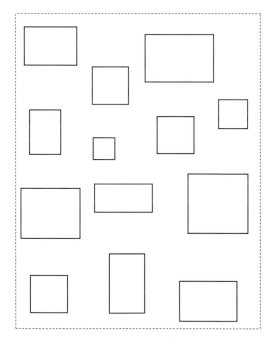

Stencilling:
Devoré curtain
pages 12–15
(photocopy and enlarge 1000%)

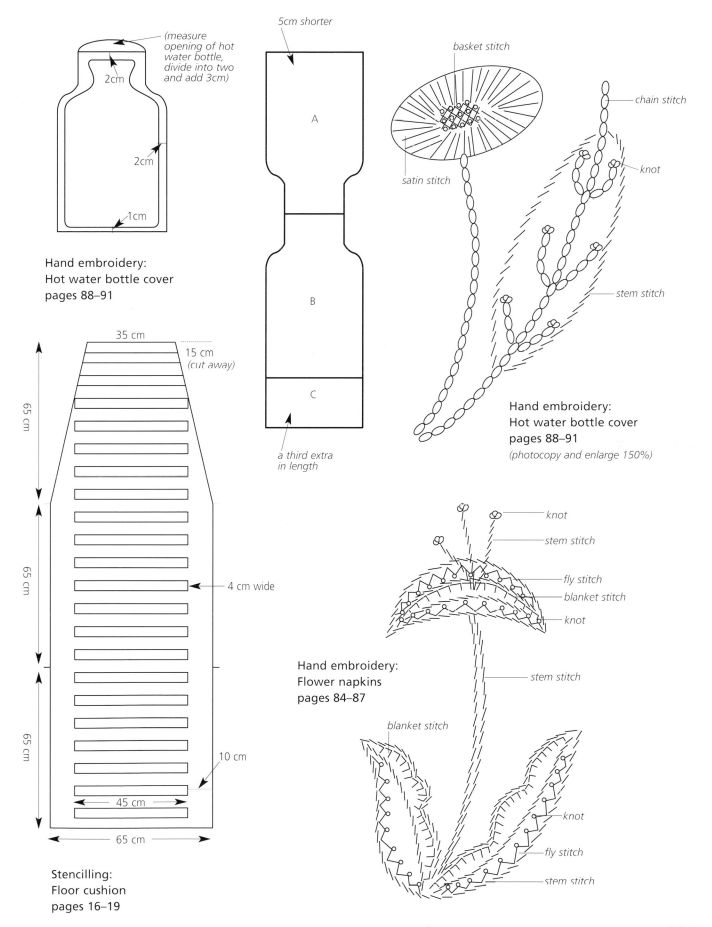

(measure opening of hot water bottle, divide into two and add 3cm)

2cm

2cm

1cm

Hand embroidery:
Hot water bottle cover
pages 88–91

5cm shorter

A

B

C

a third extra
in length

basket stitch

chain stitch

knot

satin stitch

stem stitch

Hand embroidery:
Hot water bottle cover
pages 88–91
(photocopy and enlarge 150%)

35 cm

15 cm
(cut away)

65 cm

65 cm

65 cm

4 cm wide

10 cm

45 cm

65 cm

Stencilling:
Floor cushion
pages 16–19

knot

stem stitch

fly stitch

blanket stitch

knot

blanket stitch

Hand embroidery:
Flower napkins
pages 84–87

stem stitch

knot

fly stitch

stem stitch

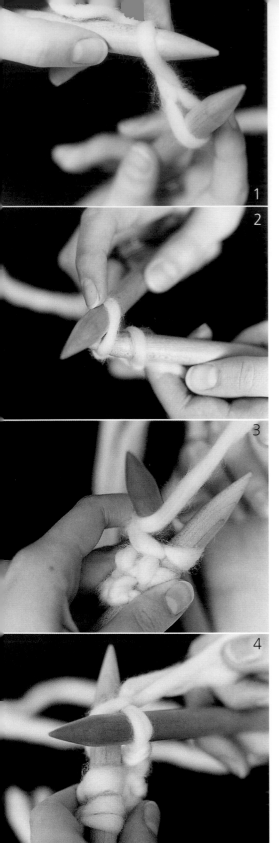

how to: Knit

Slip knot

This makes the very first stitch, before you cast on. Leaving a long end, wind the yarn around two fingers on your left hand to make a circle, then pull the yarn through the circle with the knitting needle. Pull the ends so they are fairly tight.

1 & 2 Casting on

Start with the slip knot on the left needle. Push the empty right needle throught the loop on the left hand needle, from front to back, so that it crosses behind the left needle. Wind the yarn from the ball around the point of the right needle, from below it to above it. Pull the right needle towards you and draw out the loop of the new stitch being formed. Pass the loop onto the left needle, in front of the previous stitch. Secure the stitch by pulling the yarn, but avoid pulling it too tightly. Repeat, using the first stitch on the left needle to form another new stitch, and so on until the required number of stitches has been cast on. You are ready to start knitting. The first row is a knit row.

3, 4 & 5 The knit stitch

Hold the needle with the cast-on stitches in your left hand. Push the empty (right) needle through the top of the first stitch, from front to back, so that it crosses behind the left needle. Wind the yarn from the ball around the point of the right needle, from below it to above it. Pull the right needle back and out of the cast-on stitch, still holding the yarn on its end. Drop the cast-on stitch off the end of the left needle. Repeat until you have reached the end of the row, then change the needles over.

The purl stitch

Make sure that the yarn is at the front of the needle. Holding the needle with the cast-on stitches in your left hand, push the empty (right) needle through the front of the first stitch, from front to back, so that it crosses in front of the left needle. Wind the yarn from the ball around the point of the right needle, from above it to below and back up again. Pull the right needle back and out of the cast-on stitch, still holding the yarn on its end. Drop the cast-on stitch off the end of the left needle. Repeat until you have reached the end of the row, then change the needles over.

Casting off

Knit (or purl) two stitches. Push the left needle into the first stitch that you worked on the right needle and lift it over the second stitch, and off the needle. Knit (or purl) the next stitch so that you again have two stitches on the right needle, and repeat until you have only one stitch left. Pull the yarn through this stitch to secure it.

how to: **Crochet**

To start

Hold the hook in your right hand as you would a pencil. The left hand controls the flow of the yarn from the ball and the fingers maintain the tension. Holding the ball in your left hand, pass the yarn under your little finger and around the finger in a circle; then over the third, centre and index fingers. The centre finger supports the yarn in an easy position to be picked up with the hook. The yarn circled around the little finger maintains the tension to keep the stitches even. The index finger and thumb hold the work

Slip knot

Make a loop, then hook another loop through it. Tighten gently and slide the knot up the hook.

1 & 2 Chain (ch)

Hold the slip knot between the thumb and centre finger of your left hand. Insert the hook through the loop then under the yarn, which is supported by the centre finger. Draw the yarn through the loop. This makes the first chain (1ch). Repeat this action to make as many chains as required.

3 Slip stitch (sl st)

Insert the hook into the next stitch. Catch the yarn with the hook and draw the yarn through the stitch and through the loop on the hook.

4 Double crochet (dc)

i) After making a chain, insert the hook into the 2nd ch from the hook. Wind the yarn over the hook. ii) Draw the yarn through the stitch (you should now have 2 loops on the hook). Wind the yarn over the hook again. iii) Draw through the 2 loops on the hook. There is now 1 loop on the hook and 1dc made. Continue in this way, working into each remaining ch, to the end of the row. iv) To be able to start another row, work a single ch to bring you up to the correct height. This is called a turning chain. Turn the work around, keeping the hook in the right hand. v) For the next row, insert the hook under the 2 loops at the top of the last stitch of the previous row. Continue in this way to the end of the row. Work a single ch.

5 Treble crochet (tr)

i) After making a chain, wind the yarn over the hook and insert the hook into the 4th ch from the hook ii) Draw the yarn through the stitch (you should now have 3 loops on the hook). iii) Yarn over the hook, draw the yarn through 2 loops (2 loops left on the hook). iv) Yarn over the hook again, and draw through the remaining 2 loops. There is now 1 loop on the hook and 1tr made. Continue in this way, working into each remaining ch, to the end of the row. v) To be able to start another row, work 2ch to bring you up to the correct height. This is called a turning chain. Turn the work around, keeping the hook in the right hand. vi) For the next row, insert the hook under the 2 loops at the top of the last stitch of the previous row. Continue in this way to the end of the row. Work a single ch.

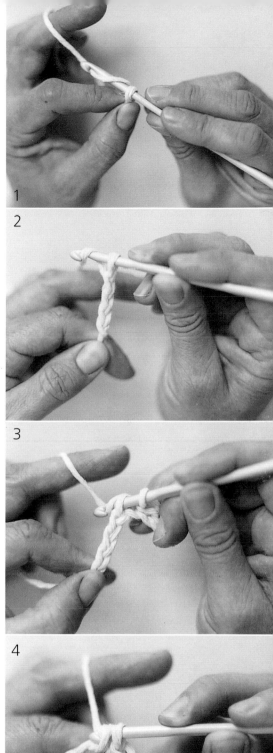

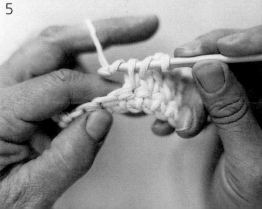

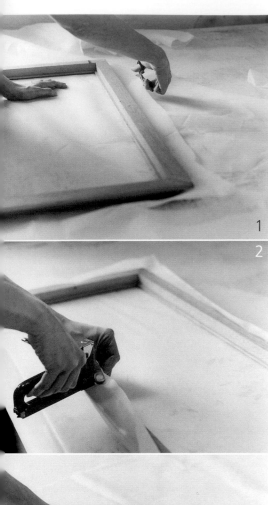

make your own: **Printing Screen and Squeegee**

to make the PRINTING SCREEN
You will need:

- A small wooden frame (such as an old picture frame or artists' stretchers, or four wooden battens)
- Polyester screen mesh about 10cm larger all round than the screen, or polyester net curtaining, or organza fabric
- Staple gun
- Scissors
- Strips of thick card
- Masking tape

1 If you are using four wooden battens, nail them together to make a sturdy frame. Stretch the mesh tightly and evenly across the frame. Staple, working from the centre of each side to the corners.

2 Trim away excess fabric. Push the strips of card between the mesh and the frame to make the mesh really taut. Tape the back of the screen to seal.

to make the SQUEEGEE
You will need:

- Wooden batten
- Calico
- Staple gun

1 Cut a batten of thin, straight, inexpensive wood to about 5cm wider than the width of your image and about 8cm less than the width of the screen frame.

2 Wrap a piece of calico around it several times to soften the edge, then staple firmly.

When you have finished printing, rip the calico off and attach a new piece for the next colour.

Contributors

STENCILLING:
TRACY KENDALL WALLPAPER

116 Greyhound Lane,
London SW16 5RN
Tel: (020) 7640 9071
Fax: (020) 8769 0618
tracy@tkendall.fsbusiness.co.uk

SCREEN PRINTING:
TRACY KENDALL WALLPAPER

116 Greyhound Lane,
London SW16 5RN
Tel: (020) 7640 9071
Fax: (020) 8769 0618
tracy@tkendall.fsbusiness.co.uk

CYANOTYPE:
BARBARA JONES

barbara.a.jones@talk21.com
Mob: 07776 455913

SILK PAINTING:
SALLY WEATHERILL

11 Queen Street, Castle
Hedingham, Essex CO9 3EK

SHIBORI:
SARA KEITH

saraakeith@aol.com

KNITTING:
CATHERINE TOUGH TEXTILES

Suite 41, 63 Jeddo Road,
London W12 9ED
Tel/fax: (020) 8743 9186

CROCHET:
ERIKA KNIGHT

26 Great College Street,
Brighton, Sussex BN2 1HL
Tel: (01273) 702 220
Mob: 07970 539319
erika@eka.demon.co.uk

HAND EMBROIDERY:
HIROKO AONO-BILLSON

28 Han Street, Richmond,
Surrey TW10 7HT
Tel/fax: (020) 8940 2961
Mob: 07855 827111

MACHINE EMBROIDERY:
ANNETTE NAUDIN

Mob: 07957 471509
annettenaudin@hotmail.com

QUILTING:
JEANNE LAINÉ

1 Cleveland House, Hackford Road,
London SW9 0ET
Tel: (020) 7582 3420

APPLIQUÉ:
LISA VAUGHAN

Unit 258, The Clerkenwell
Workshops, 27–31 Clerkenwell
Close, London EC1R 0AT
Tel/fax: (020) 7250 0085
LVT@handbag.com

COMPLEX TEXTILES:
CORINNE PIERRE

Sycamore Cottage, Midway,
Chalford Hill, Gloucestershire
GL6 8EN, Tel: 01453 731 223
Mob: 07977 574 895
corinne@netgates.co.uk

FELT MAKING:
MARY KIRK

Studio 21, Great Western Studios,
Great Western Road, London
W9 3NY, Tel: (020) 7286 9530
Fax: (020) 8960 3924;
mary-kirk@bigfoot.com

USING FELT:
ANNE KYYRÖ QUINN

Tel: (020) 7486 2561
annekyyrodesign@aol.com

WEAVING:
Salt. ®

OXO Tower, Bargehouse Street,
London SE1 9PH, Tel: (020) 7593
0007, Fax: (020) 7401 6404
enquiries@salt-uk.com
www.salt-uk.com

RIBBONWORK:
HIKARU NOGUCHI TEXTILE DESIGN

Unit 2L, Cockpit Workshops,
Cockpit Yard, London WC1N 2NP
Tel: (020) 7813 1227
Fax: (020) 7813 0883

BEADWORK:
KAREN SPURGIN

39 Sundorne Road, London SE7 7PR
Tel: (020) 8355 4729
www.spurgin.co.uk

BASKETRY:
LIZZIE FAREY

8 Threave Road, Rhonehouse,
Castle Douglas DG7 1TD, Scotland
Tel/fax: (01556) 680473
lfarey@talk21.com

PAPER MAKING:
DAVID WATSON

Tel: (01273) 505201
d.a.watson@virgin.net

PAPIER MÂCHÉ:
CLAIRE ATTRIDGE

12 Ellicott Road, Horfield,
Bristol BS7 9PT
claire@attridge.co.uk

PAPERCRAFT:
ALEXANDRA GOUGH

Tel: (020) 7582 3420

CERAMIC PAINTING:
VICTORIA BRYAN

19, Northdown Avenue, Cliftonville,
Margate, Kent, CT9 2NL,
Tel: (01843) 227 494,
Fax: (01843) 297 919,
victoriabryan@hotmail.com

GLASS PAINTING:
KATE MAESTRI

Studio 2.11, Oxo Tower Wharf,
Bargehouse Street, London SE1 9PH
Tel: (020) 7620 0330
Fax: (020) 7928 9759

MOSAIC:
DONNA REEVES

33a Kay Road, London SW9 9DF
Tel: (020) 7733 7060
Fax: (020) 7737 0761
Mob: 07770 886 764

GILDING:
JANE CASSINI AND SANDRA LEE

SILVERWORK:
AMANDA DOUGHTY

Studio 2, Cockpit Workshops,
Cockpit Yard, Northington St, London
WC1N 2NP, Tel: (020) 7831 7390,
amanda@amandadoughty.com
www.amandadoughty.com

WIREWORK:
GEORGIE GLEN

SOAP MAKING:
SUE FLOCKHART

sue_flockhart@hotmail.com

PLASTIC DESIGN:
KATHIE MURPHY

1B Oldfield Road, London N16 0RR
Mob: 07973 249 852
Fax: (020) 7254 9528

ACRYLIC MOULDING:
MARLENE MCKIBBIN

118 Forest Road, London E8 3BH
Tel/fax: (020) 7683 0931

Suppliers

UK

STENCILLING

Alma Leather *12–14 Greatorex Street, London E1 5NF; Tel: (020) 7375 0343*

Pongees *(for silk organza and silk viscose for devoré) 28 Hoxton Square, London N1 6NN; Tel: (020) 7739 9130*

Suasion *(for all dyes and chemicals) The Studios, 1 Stevenage Road, Knebworth, Herts, SG3 6AN; Tel: (01438) 815 252 www.suasion-uk.com*

Tempo Leather *Congreve Street, London SE17 1TJ; Tel: (020) 7252 7032*

Walter Reginald Group Ltd *(for leather and suede) Unit 6, 100 The Highway, London E1 9BX; Tel: (020) 7481 2233*

Whaleys (Bradford) Ltd *(for silk organza and silk viscose for devoré and other fabrics) Harris Court, Great Horton, Bradford, W. Yorkshire BD7 4E8; Tel: (01274) 576 718; www.whaleysofbradford.co.uk*

SCREEN PRINTING

CSL *(for silkscreens, squeegees, mixed coating emulsions to paint on silkscreens) Jaycee House, Croydon Business Centre, 214 Purley Way, Croydon, Surrey CR0 4X9; Tel: (020) 8256 1500*

Pongees, Suasion, Whaleys *(see Stencilling)*

CYANOTYPE

B&Q *(for lampshades) Call 0845 300 2897 for branches*

Borovick Fabrics *16 Berwick St, London W1V 4HP; Tel: (020) 7437 2180*

John Lewis *(for fabrics and haberdashery) Oxford St, London W1 1EX; Tel: (020) 7629 7711*

London Graphic Centre *(for watercolour paper) 16–18 Shelton St, London WC2 9NT; Tel: (020) 7759 4500*

MacCulloch & Wallis *(for fabrics) 25–26 Dering St, London W1R 0BH; Tel: (020) 7629 0311*

Pentonville Rubber *(for foam) Pentonville Rd, London N1; Tel: (020) 7837 7553*

R&L Slaughter Ltd *(for chemicals) Units 11 & 12 Upminster Trading Park, Warley St, Upminster, Essex RM14 3PJ; Tel: (01708) 227 140*

SILK PAINTING

Pongees, Suasion, Whaleys *(see Stencilling)*

SHIBORI

George Weil and Fibrecrafts *(for dyes, fabrics and books) Old Portsmouth Road, Peasmarsh, Guildford, Surrey, GU3 1LZ; Tel: (01483) 565 800 (mail order)*

Kemtex Services Ltd *(for dyes) Tameside Business Centre, Windmill Lane, Denton, Manchester, M34 3QS; Tel: (0161) 320 6505*

Whaleys *(see Stencilling)*

Wholesale fabrics *(for fabrics prepared for dyeing) Tel: (01274) 576 718 (mail order)*

KNITTING

Wingham Wool Work *Freepost, Wentworth, Rotherham, South Yorks, SG2 7TN; Tel: (01226) 742 926; www.winghamwoolwork.co.uk*

CROCHET

Jaeger *(for yarn) Tel: (01325) 339 4237*

Muji *(for string) Tel: (020) 7823 8688; www.mujionline.com*

Rowan *(for yarn) Green Lane Mill, Holmfirth HD9 2DX England; Tel: (01484) 681 881; www.knitrowan.com*

Sirdar *(for yarn) www.merribee.com*

Woolworths *(for strings) Tel: 0845 608 1102*

HAND EMBROIDERY

The Cloth Shop *290 Portobello Road, London W10 5TE; Tel: (020) 8968 6001*

John Lewis *(see Cyanotype)*

MACHINE EMBROIDERY

Barn Yarns *Tel: 0870 870 8586; www.barnyarns.com*

MacCulloch & Wallis *(see Cyanotype)*

QUILTING

John Lewis *(see Cyanotype)*

APPLIQUÉ

Ian Mankin *(for fabric) 109 Regents Park Road, London NW1 8UR; Tel: (020) 7722 0997*

The Bead Shop *(for beads, nylon, threads and findings) 21A Tower Street, London WC2 9NS; Tel: (020) 7240 0931*

Whaleys *(see Stencilling)*

COMPLEX TEXTILES

Corinne Pierre *(for glass inserts) (see p331)*

Dylon *(for dyes) www.dylon.com*

Wolfin Textiles *359 Uxbridge Road, Hatch End, Middlesex HA5 4JN; Tel: (020) 8428 9911;*

FELT MAKING

The Handweavers Gallery and Studio *(for wool fibre) 29 Haroldstone Road, London, E17 7AN; Tel: (020) 8521 2281; www.handweaversstudio.co.uk*

USING FELT

B Brown Display Materials *(for display felt) Tel: 08705 340 340*

The Handweavers Studio & Gallery Ltd *(see Felt Making)*

Naish Felts Ltd *Crow Lane, Wilton, Salisbury, Wiltshire SP2 0HB; Tel: (01722) 743 505*

WEAVING

John Lewis *(see Cyanotype)*

The Scientific Wire Company *18 Raven Road, London, E18 1HW; Tel: (020) 8505 0002; Fax: (020) 8559 1114*

RIBBONWORK

The Bead Shop *(see Appliqué)*

John Lewis *(see Cyanotype)*

VV Rouleaux *(for ribbon) 54 Cliveden Place, London SW1 8AX; Tel: (020) 7730 3125*

BEADWORK

The Bead Shop *(see Appliqué)*

John Lewis *(see Cyanotype)*

MacCulloch & Wallis *(see Cyanotype)*

VV Rouleaux *(see Ribbonwork)*

Silken Strands *(for thread for machine and hand embroidery) 20Y Rhos Gwynedd, Bangor LL57 2LT; Tel: (01248) 362 361; www.silkenstrands.co.uk*

BASKETRY

PH Coate & Son *(for willow) Meave Green Court, Stoke St Gregory, Taunton, Somerset TA3 6HY; Tel: (01823) 490 249*

EM & HJ Lock *(for willow) Lockleaze, Thorney Road, Kingsbury Episcopi, Mattock, Somerset TA12 6BQ; Tel: (01935) 823 338*

PAPER MAKING

E. Ploton *(for specialist artists' materials) Tel: (020) 8348 0315; www.ploton.co.uk*

(plus Oriental supermarkets for wheat starch)

PAPERCRAFT

Ordning and Reda *(for notebooks and albums) 186A Kings Road, London SW3 5XP; Tel: (020) 7351 1003*

Paperchase *(for a wide selection of papers) www.paperchase.co.uk*

CERAMIC PAINTING

Pebeo *(for ceramic paints)*
Tel: (02380) 701 144 for stockists;
www.pebeo.com

GLASS PAINTING

Lead and Light *(for glass paints)*
35a Hartland Road, London NW1 8DP;
Tel: (020) 7485 0997 (mail order)

MOSAIC

Edgar Udny & Co Ltd *(for mosaic equipment)*
314 Balham High Road, London SW17 7AA;
Tel: (020) 8767 8181

Reed Harris *(for ceramic and stone tiles)*
Riverside House, 27 Carnwath Road, London
SW6 3HR; Tel: (020) 7736 7511

GILDING

Connoisseur Studios *Hertfordshire;*
Tel: (01727) 874 488

Cornelissen and Son *(for gilding equipment)*
105 Great Russell Street, London WC1B 3RY;
Tel (020) 7636 1045; www.cornelissen.com

Go Glass *127 Cherry Hinton Road, Cambridge;*
Tel: (01223) 211 041

Heffers Art & Graphics *15 King St, Cambridge;*
Tel: (01223) 568 495

SILVERWORK

The Bead Shop *(see Appliqué)*

Cooksons & Exchange Findings *(for findings,*
settings and tools); Tel: 0121 200 2120;
www.cooksongold.com

Earring Things *Craft Workshops, South Pier*
Road, Ellesmere Port, Cheshire CH65 4FW;
Tel: (0151) 356 4444; www.beadmaster.com

Ells & Farrier/Creative Beadcraft *20 Beak*
Street, London W1R 3HA; Tel: (020) 7629 9964

Kaleidoscope Crafts *3 Grove Park, Brislington,*
Bristol BS4 3LG (mail order only)

SOAP MAKING

Aroma Trading Limited *(for essential oils)*
Chapel Farm, Hartwell, Northampton, England,
NN7 2EU; Tel: (01908) 511 881;
e-mail sales@aromatrading.com;
www.aromatrading.co.uk

The Handmade Natural Soap Company
(for a range of soap making supplies)
2d Maryland, Wells Next the Sea, Norfolk,
NR23 1LY; Tel: (01328) 711 717
e-mail: sphillips@strange.co.uk
www.strange.co.uk/soap

More than Soap
(for soap base, moulds & other soap making
items) Llys Aeron, Penrhyncoch, Aberystwyth,
Ceredigion, SY23 3EP; Tel: (01970) 820 858;
e-mail: nia@morethansoap.co.uk;
www.morethansoap.co.uk

Phoenix Natural Products Ltd
(for essential oils and other goods) Unit 15
Witley Industrial Estate, Witley Gardens, Southall,
Middlesex, UB2 4EZ; Tel: 020 8574 7308;
e-mail: Info@PhoenixUK.com; www.phoenixuk.com

PLASTIC DESIGN

Alec Tiranti Ltd
(for sculptors' tools and equipment) 70 High
Street, Theale, Reading RG7 5AR;
Tel: (0118) 930 2775; or 20 Warren Street,
London W1P 5DG; Tel: (020) 7636 8565;
www.tiranti.co.uk

Trylon Ltd
(for model casting and enamelling supplies)
Thrift Street, Wollaston, Northamptonshire
NN29 7QJ; Tel: (01933) 664 275

ACRYLIC MOULDING

The Bead Shop *(see Appliqué)*

Dylon *(see Complex Textiles)*

The Publisher would also like to give special
thanks to the following companies for the
generous use of props:

291 Antiques *291 Lillie Road, London SW6 5PY*
Tel: (020) 7381 5008

New Heights *1–3 Lavender Hill, London SW11*
5QW, (020) 7622 4744; www.new-heights.co.uk

Artefact *303 Munster Road, London SW6 6BJ;*
Tel: (020) 7610 2724

The Conran Shop *Michelin House, 81 Fulham*
Road, London SW3 6RD; Tel: (020) 7589 7401;
www.conran.com

Geoffrey Harris Lighting Ltd *537 Battersea*
Park Rd, London SW11 3BL; (020) 7228 6101

The Iron Bed Company *580 Fulham Road,*
London SW6 5NT; Tel: (020) 7610 9903;
www.ironbed.co.uk

Judy Greenwood Antiques *657 Fulham Road,*
London SW6 5PY; Tel: (020) 7736 6037

The White Company *8 Symons Street, London,*
SW3 2TJ; Tel: 0870 160 1610;
www.thewhiteco.com

AUSTRALIA
GENERAL CRAFT

Country Bumpkin *88 Fullarton Road,*
Norwood SA 5067; Tel: (08) 8363 4544;
www.countrybumpkin.com.au

Craft Smart *4/29 Business Park Drive,*
Notting Hill Vic. 3168; Tel: (03) 9558 9477;
www.craftsmart.com.au

Lincraft Stores nationwide *31–33 Alfred*
Street, Blackburn Vic. 3130; Tel: 1800 640 107
or (03) 9875 7575

Spotlight Stores nationwide
Reply Paid 72483, South Melbourne Vic. 3205;
Tel: 1300 305 405 or (03) 9684 7625
www.spotlight.com.au

STENCILLING

KraftKolour Pty Ltd *(for devoré paint)*
242 High St, Northcote Vic. 3070
Tel: (03) 9482 9234

CYANOTYPE

Vanbar Photographic & Digital Supplies
(for chemicals for cyanotyping) stores in Carlton
(Vic.), South Yarra (Vic.), Glebe (NSW), Vanbar
Pty Ltd, 159 Cardigan St, Carlton Vic. 3053,
Tel: (03) 9347 7788; www.vanbar.com.au

KNITTING

Colored Jules Wool on the Web *PO Box 16*
Drysdale Vic. 3222; Tel: (03) 5251 1677;
www.coloredjules.com.au

HAND/MACHINE EMBROIDERY

Tapestry Craft *32 York Street, Sydney NSW 2000*
Tel: (02) 9299 8588; www.tapestrycraft.com.au

RIBBONWORK

Scarlet Ribbons Needlecraft *45 Kirwan Street,*
Floreat WA 6014; Tel: (08) 9383 9073

BEADWORK

The Bead Company of Australia Stores
Chatswood, Enmore and Hurstville, PO Box 243,
Hurstville NSW 1481; Tel: (02) 9580 4923;
www.beadcompany.com.au

PAPERCRAFT

Papercraft Australia *16 Valediction Road,*
Kings Park NSW 2148; Tel: (02) 9672 3888

CERAMIC PAINTING

Jazz It Up Ceramics *483 Crown Street,*
Surry Hills NSW 2010; Tel: (02) 8394 9499;
www.jazzitup.com.au

Index

First published in 2002 by Murdoch Books UK Ltd
Copyright© 2002 Murdoch Books UK Ltd

ISBN 1 85391 963 2
A catalogue record for this book is available from the British Library.

Commissioning Editor: **Natasha Martyn-Johns**
Project Editor: **Dawn Henderson**
Design and Art Direction: **Cathy Layzell**
Managing Editor: **Anna Osborn**
Design Manager: **Helen Taylor**
Photo Librarian: **Bobbie Leah**
Photographer: **Howard Sooley**
Stylist: **Rebecca de Boehmler**
with additional styling by **Emeline Hudson**
Illustrator: **Christopher King**

CEO: **Robert Oerton**
Publisher: **Catie Ziller**
Production Manager: **Lucy Byrne**
International Sales Director: **Kevin Lagden**

Colour separation by Colourscan
Printed in China by Toppan Printing

Murdoch Books UK Ltd
Ferry House, 51–57 Lacy Road
Putney, London SW15 1PR
United Kingdom
Tel: +44 (0)20 8355 1480
Fax: +44 (0)20 8355 1499
Murdoch Books UK Ltd is a subsidiary
of Murdoch Magazines Pty Ltd

UK Distribution
Macmillan Distribution Ltd
Houndsmills, Brunell Road
Basingstoke, Hampshire, RG1 6XS
United Kingdom
Tel: +44 (0) 1256 302 707
Fax: +44 (0) 1256 351 437
http://www.macmillan-mdl.co.uk

Murdoch Books®
GPO Box 1203
Sydney NSW 1045
Australia
Tel: +61 (0)2 8220 2000
Fax: +61 (0)2 8220 2020
Murdoch Books® is a trademark
of Murdoch Magazines Pty Ltd